The French Canadians,
1759 - 1766;
Conquered?
Half - Conquered?
Liberated?

ISSUES IN CANADIAN HISTORY

General Editor
MORRIS ZASLOW

Other Volumes in Preparation:

French Canada and the Struggle for Responsible Government

Upper Canada Toryism

The United Empire Loyalists

The Constitutional Crises and Election of 1926

The Expulsion of the Acadians

William Lyon Mackenzie—the Man and His Work

Joseph Howe in Nova Scotia Politics

Centralist Ideas of the Fathers of Confederation

Mackenzie King as a Social Reformer

ISSUES

IN

CANADIAN
HISTORY

The French Canadians, 1759-1766: Conquered? Half-Conquered? Liberated?

Translated, edited and selected by
CAMERON NISH

THE COPP CLARK PUBLISHING COMPANY

VANCOUVER   TORONTO   MONTREAL

To Holly

ISBN 0 7730 3105 7

[1496]

Foreword

Is there a dearth of discussion and controversy in Canadian historical writing? Does such a lack partially explain why so many accept and proclaim the view that Canadian history is unrelievedly dull? Has the writing of history in Canada reached the point where important issues may be presented to the public in depth? These are some of the questions that have inspired the publication of ISSUES IN CANADIAN HISTORY. By means of its volumes the series aims to encourage wider, franker discussions of historical problems and to stimulate a revisionist approach to the entire range of Canadian history.

ISSUES IN CANADIAN HISTORY aims to publish some twenty or twenty-five volumes, dealing with a corresponding number of significant problems. Each volume will represent a balance between contemporary documents illustrating the problem (statutes, policy statements, commentaries) and latter-day reviews and evaluations drawn from periodicals and specialized works. Each is being prepared by a specialist in the particular area who, in addition to selecting and arranging the excerpts, is responsible for the introductions and a bibliographic essay.

Teachers have long felt a need for such a series, in which the most significant features of an important topic are collected between the covers of a single, not too expensive book of moderate size. Though the series is intended primarily for the university, the separate volumes will prove invaluable to high school classes and for general readers seeking to broaden their historical background.

An examination of contemporary documents will reveal how the participants viewed and reacted to the situations they faced; permitting the student, through an act of historical imagination, to feel some-thing of the immediacy of the events, and breathe life into the forgotten past. He will receive training in historical techniques, through being given the opportunity to observe how the historian reconstructs an occurrence, how he marshals his evidence, how he shapes his conclusions. He may learn how the historian's conclusions were affected by the materials he selected, and how historians may arrive at different conclusions from the same body of evidence. He may gain an insight into those eternal historiographic problems—what really happened? what was the true meaning of those happenings? how did the historians reach their conclusions? The student may discover that there is more than one answer to a historical question, that he need not accept conclusions ready-made but is free to reach his own. Eventually he may come to feel the pleasures of sitting in judgment upon the past, of being his own historian.

Hopefully, such studies may help to efface the unfortunate notion of Canadian history as an undiscerning, arid collecting of factual details for their own sake. Instead, the reader may glimpse the enlightening and liberating concept of a lively, many-faceted history; of a discipline which, while drawing upon other scholarly disciplines, verges upon a creative art in its tasks of careful analysis, imaginative synthesis, judicious evaluation, and sympathetic assessment.

For the historian, too, ISSUES IN CANADIAN HISTORY furnishes a new approach. Each volume is intended to bring forward an important, fundamental problem from Canada's past, expressed through the medium of a wide range of documents and the most diversified and distinguished group of modern studies available. The volumes focus upon major aspects of Canadian history, and each abounds in conflicts and controversies. They cast a searching light upon versions and interpretations which have been accepted uncritically for far too many years.

By revealing the sometimes inadequate levels of past performances, these volumes may some day expose present-day historians to an audience more qualified to criticize their assumptions and preconceptions, while at the same time they make the historians more aware of the foundations of their own thought. Thus enlightened, they may become bolder in taking controversial positions, inspiring arguments and counter-arguments which demonstrate that Canadian historical problems often are very equivocal, subtle and complex.

ISSUES IN CANADIAN HISTORY hopes to encourage the study and writing of history in Canada to advance to a higher, more sophisticated, more intellectually demanding level; to show that many topics in Canadian history possess diversity, breadth, intellectual sparkle, and profundity; and to demonstrate that Canadian history, properly understood by those who make the effort, is far from being dull.

M. Zaslow

May, 1966

Contents

Introduction

What happens when a country is conquered? This simple, categorical question has been, and is presently being, disputed by Canadian historians of the English and French languages. A. R. M. Lower, in his *Colony to Nation*, has called a conquest "a type of slavery" and added that a "Conquest, like slavery, must be experienced to be understood."[1] A very, very different historian, the aged Canon Lionel Groulx, has cited Lower, and one can almost hear the venerable Canon murmuring *bien, bien*.[2] François-Xavier Garneau, a man responsible, perhaps above all others, for the creation of *nationaliste* history in French Canada, brutally called the period immediately after the Conquest a *tyranny*. A past president of the Canadian Historical Association, and one of the foremost contemporary historians of French Canada, Marcel Trudel, called the same period *highly laudable*.[3] William Smith, a historian of the last century, claimed that the French of Canada were well rid of their despotic French masters. The chief spokesman of the *Conquest Hypothesis*, Michel Brunet, views the Conquest as a disaster; the origins of the alienation of the French Canadians, and the main reason for their present inferiority in modern Canada. Fernand Ouellet, a younger contemporary of Michel Brunet, disagrees: the French Canadians, before and after the Conquest, were inferior to the English in political and economic institutions, hence their present position.[4]

One of the evident, and odd, features of the controversy over the Conquest and

---

[1]—A. R. M. Lower, *Colony to Nation*, p. 63.
[2]—Lionel Groulx, *Histoire du Canada Français*, vol. III, p. 8.
[3]—See Part II, *below.*
[4]—See Parts I and VII, *below.*

1

the early period of the British regime is that the problem cannot be neatly divided along national lines: the French Canadian historians versus the Anglo-Canadian (or more pejorative) Anglo-Saxon historians. Lower and Ouellet have more in common than Brunet and Ouellet; A. L. Burt and Thomas Chapais honor the conqueror while F.-X. Garneau chastises him. The French Canadian Catholic, Marcel Trudel, is more critical of the Church in the period 1760 to 1766 than is the Anglo-Canadian Protestant Hilda Neatby. The problem, then, is a matter of historical and not merely national controversy. Let us again ask: what happens to a country when it is conquered?

Quebec, the impregnable fortress, capitulated in 1759. Inland, the metropolis of Montreal remained to the French until 1760. The Peace of Paris of 1763 confirmed the victories of the British arms. The temporary Military Regime lasted until October 1764 when Murray, as Governor-General, became the head of the first civil government under British rule. This bare recital leaves unanswered the basic question: what happens to a country when it is conquered?

Two hundred and more years have passed since that decisive event. We no longer see the bombed, shattered and crumbling walls of the town of Quebec. The wasted fields and the hungry cattle are *romantic* items of the *past*. The famine and cold of the 65,000 or so inhabitants of New France are history. The fears, uncertainties and hopes of the past are muted; they are words in a book.

The British soldiers and the mercenaries from Europe, after a long, hard war, were victorious, and received the plaudits of the English press. The British-Americans, the colonials, after more than fifty years

of skirmishing, had achieved, finally, a singular victory. They, above all others among the conquering armies, had felt the bite and pain of the Indians' tomahawks and arrows; they, above all others, bled from wounds inflicted by the French regulars and Canadian militia. To them, the massacres and propaganda were not words but actions, realities, which resulted often enough, too often, in the death of their parents, their children and their wives. This is the personal equation. There is another.

The conquest of Canada was a many-faceted event. To the British government, it meant a period of imperial reorganization. The last war, the Seven Years War, or as it was known in America, the French and Indian War, had been expensive. Money was required to pay for it. It was, for the times, an international war fought in Europe, India and America. It gained for the Empire lands, new lands with foreign populations, new lands which had to be incorporated and administered by and from London.

The Conquest, for the citizens of Massachusetts, New York, Pennsylvania, and other British colonies in America, held a different meaning: finally, the hated Papist enemy had been brought to his knees. The New York fur traders looked forward to exploitation of the rich resources of the recently acquired hinterland. This, to them, was a major problem which the British government should resolve in their favour. In Pennsylvania and Virginia great expanses of virgin soil west of the Alleghenies awaited them and, of course, the profits from the sale and cultivation of the lands. The coastal trade and fishing of the Massachusetts resident would no longer have to fear the French installations at Louisbourg. To the American colonists, the post-war period was a colonial problem; to their masters, the British, it was a colonial and an imperial problem.

The inhabitants of the colony of New France in 1759 and 1760 did not know what to expect. They literally feared summary execution, for had not their government told them to expect no mercy from the enemy? Would they remain French? This hope existed till 1763. If they became members of another state, what would happen to the property they held? the language they spoke? the faith they held and practised? the millions of *livres* of card money which they had received from the now defeated French state? Would they be deported as had been the Acadians? Would they be permitted to leave the country? Should they return to France? These were their immediate concerns.

Two other groups, less numerous, but because of the Conquest, significant, were the British administrators and the British or British-American merchants. These last established themselves at the invitation of the former in the newly conquered lands, engaged in commerce, and on the basis of promises given by the British administrators made Canada their homeland. The administrators had to establish British power in a land and among a people long hostile to the *protestants, British*, and as they called the American colonials, the *Bostonians*. The British army, the British administrators and the new immigrants (but called *Old Subjects*) were a decided minority numerically, yet they held all power. What to do?

Today it is simple to see what should and should not have been done. Then, in 1759 and the years that followed, the many elements—the Imperial authorities in London, the American colonists, the French Canadians, the British administrators, and the *Old Subjects*—did not possess our wisdom, based as it is upon their *successes* and their *failures*. Yet, with all our hindsight, knowledge and vast documentation, we still are not sure of the significance of the period. We know what happened, and to some extent, why it happened. We are even capable of assessing some of its present significance. But its ultimate significance is questionable; it is still current history. Our point of departure, our interrogative hypothesis remains: what happens to a country when it is conquered?

Clash of Opinion

"The haste of the conquered to submit to the authority of a century-old enemy, their docility, the servility of their ruling classes, surprises a twentieth-century observer a little. . . . The words "collaboration" and "collaborators" have a very bad press in our day."

MICHEL BRUNET

"The decision . . . to keep Canada . . . has never been fully explained."

MARJORIE G. REID

"The military heel has ground out groans from conquered people in many lands. But the rule of the soldier . . . was particularly light in Canada . . ."

A. L. BURT

"This pitiful picture of these people in 1760 is of more than ephemeral interest. It is one of the most important and abiding things in Canadian history, for the glorious contrast presented by the conditions of their children in successive generations has been and will continue to be the chief inspiration of the French Canadian race."

A. L. BURT

"Open your eyes, Canadians, to your own interests, . . . We exhort you eagerly to have recourse to a people, free, honest and generous. . . . For if you do not profit by this advice, you must expect the most rigorous treatment . . ."

PROCLAMATION BY MURRAY, 1759

"Gentlemen, turning your eyes for a moment from this sad scene, would you leap forward the space of a century? We are in Quebec. . . . A happy crowd rushes towards the historic site of the old episcopal palace . . . where another building consecrated to the deliberations of an autonomous legislature stands. . . . And this governor . . . is a man of the French race and language . . ."

THOMAS CHAPAIS

"The conquerors, having achieved their precious conquest, occupied themselves with the means of conserving it . . . Canada was treated as a barbarous nation . . ."

F.-X. GARNEAU

"Seen in this light, the military regime of the Government of Three Rivers seems to us a highly laudable regime, and it appears to merit even more eulogies . . ."

MARCEL TRUDEL

4

"During the debates on the *Quebec Act* the attempt was made to attribute the policy of 1763 to haste and inadvertence. Evidence to the contrary is to be found in a score of documents . . ."

CHESTER MARTIN

". . . the Royal Proclamation of October 7, 1763, . . . was one of the most casual and inadequate instruments of government in the history of colonial rule."

W. S. WALLACE

". . . Briand('s) . . . great task was to work within the church for order and discipline and zeal, he was always acutely conscious of the problem of relations with the secular power."

HILDA NEATBY

"On the 10th of August 1764, there began for the Church of Canada a regime of servitude under a Protestant government."

MARCEL TRUDEL

". . . the situation of Canada in the French empire, . . . is the only epoch in our history when separatism was rooted in reality."

MAURICE SÉGUIN

"One can understand the significance of this interpretation. Here the essential foundations of the *drama of the Conquest* and its tragic consequences are outlined."

FERNAND OUELLET

"The Conquest of 1760 was the cause of a social disintegration."

PHILIPPE GARIGUE

"The absence of that secular and bourgeois directing class, whose rôle has been so important . . . remains the great fact of the history of French Canada since the Conquest . . ."

MICHEL BRUNET

". . . the annihilation of the French Canadian bourgeoisie in 1760 became the great historical event which dominates and determines the economic development of French Canada until Confederation.

The thesis is seductive, but does it correspond to the exact reality? . . . the hypothesis had been advanced without any thorough research to support it. Hence the dossier is not closed; . . ."

JEAN HAMELIN

Part I

The Conquest

Controversy in history can be of at least two kinds: firstly, that engaged in by the historical personages of the period being studied, as for example, the dispute whether to keep Canada or return it to France; and secondly, the interpretation of the period by historians distant from the events they describe and explain. This Part places more emphasis on the first sort of controversy, although some of the interpretative differences, Burt and Chapais versus Brunet, will also be found. History, as E. H. Carr has written, is a dialogue between the present and the past. For the moment, let the past speak to us by concentrating on the conditions and the problems facing the conquered and the conqueror in the early years of the 1760's.

The first two selections, those of Burt and Lower, are from the pens of men noted for their sympathy for the French Canadians. The former provides a broad view of the period; he anchors the early years. His writings correct an earlier historical approach (that of William Kingsford, for example), that tended to evaluate these early years of the British Regime as merely a first step in what has so aptly been called "the paper-strewn path to Confederation." Lower's opinion of this era is not quite so rosy as that of Burt: a conquest is a rather severe event in the history of a people. But Lower implicitly and explicitly also views the Conquest as performing a service to the *Canadiens*—it freed the citizens of New France from an absolutist, mercantilist and retrogressive power, France.

Thomas Chapais, understandably, is also sympathetic to the French Canadians. In the historiography of French Canada he is classed as a moderate *nationaliste*, a euphemism for pro-British. He sketches a darker picture than does Burt, but leads us

6

to a happier vision, the colourful and triumphant days of July, 1867. Also notable in Chapais is the rôle he assigns to the Church, a rôle which loomed large in the early years of the British Regime, and which will be examined more fully in Part VI. Another *nationaliste*, but not so moderate, is Michel Brunet, the Chairman of the Department of History of the *Université de Montréal*. His analysis of the "First Reactions" of the *Canadiens* after the Conquest, which Brunet explains as a moral conquest, differs somewhat from the previous selections. The people were paralysed, uncertain and above all, alienated, no longer masters of their own fate. Brunet asks and investigates not merely what the British did, but also explains what happened by positing the choices, the alternatives faced by the *Canadiens*.

Burt, Lower, Chapais and Brunet all wrote of an event that had taken place: the retention of Canada by the British. As M. G. Reid points out, the decision to keep Canada was not always such a foregone matter. Stanley Ryerson's views on the conquest of New France and England's decision to keep the colony rest on seldom-encountered criteria in Canadian historiography: a Marxian frame of analysis. Both Reid and Ryerson place an emphasis upon imperial relations, one relatively neglected in the other selections. The significance of the conquest of New France in terms of the American colonies was appreciated before the outbreak of the American Revolution. The resolution of the imperial problem by the disintegration of the First British Empire, however, was not.

A. L. Burt, *The Old Province of Quebec,* (Minneapolis, University of Minnesota Press, 1933), pp. 1-12. Reprinted by permission of the author.

The Colony

Surrendered

The Canada that Governor Vaudreuil surrendered to the British commander-in-chief on September 8, 1760, was as large in territory as it was small in population. It extended down the Ohio, it included the Great Lakes, and no one knew how far it reached toward the setting sun. Most of this country land was still as wild as it was on the day two centuries earlier when Jacques Cartier first sailed from St. Malo to discover the land that was to be New France. To gather furs and to block the English, the French had flung their posts far and wide. But in all the great heart of the continent their only settlements were at Detroit and on the Mississippi in what was known as the Illinois country, and these were very feeble. Detroit, which belonged to Canada, contained only a thousand persons. The other community, an offshoot from Louisiana, may have had a few more. Most of the people living in these two places were limited to a primitive existence, for they had little contact with the outside world.

Only on the lower St. Lawrence had the French planted themselves in any numbers. There some sixty-two thousand Canadians inhabited a long narrow colony that stretched for two hundred and fifty miles from the southwest to the northeast. Checked by the rapids on either side of the Ottawa's mouth, settlement had climbed no farther up the St. Lawrence River than Cedars; downstream, it died out in the harsher climate of Kamouraska, which lies more than two degrees farther north. The band of settlement had no breadth except at the upper end, where it spread across the fertile islands of Jesus and Montreal and over to the right bank of the Richelieu, which runs nearly parallel to the St. Lawrence until it empties into it at Sorel. Below this point, settlement clung to the banks of the great river, here and there thrusting a little arm five or six miles up a tributary stream. On either side the river the wandering line of white cottages, built of stone or of rough-hewn timber, with now and then a church and a mill, presented the appearance of an interminable village, for the habitants' farms were squeezed together along the water's edge. Only the lower ends were cultivated. The rest of the land was left a wilderness, because it was less fertile and less accessible from the river, and, more important still, because there was no need to bring it under the plough. There was little market for agricultural produce; the seignior's dues were very light; the church's tithe was only one twenty-sixth; and there were no taxes. Most habitants, therefore, though they had large families, raised small crops. A surplus would have been a superfluity.

They led a primitive life, though not quite so primitive as that of their brethren farther west. They sold little and bought little, for almost all their food, clothing, and furniture were of home manufacture. Nor was their independence confined to material things. They knew nothing of the weight of civilization which bore so heavily upon the lower orders at home. No deep social gulf separated them from their feudal lords, the seigniors, and many of these, indeed, were little better off than themselves. European travelers had already observed that they "breathed from their birth the air of liberty," and that "even the ordinary habitants lived in greater ease and comfort than did thousands of the gentlemen of France," for privilege sickens whereas freedom and equality thrive in a pioneer atmosphere. The habitants' relations with the church were friendly and intimate, because the parish clergy were drawn mostly from their own ranks. And the church itself, imbued with the missionary zeal of frontier life, preserved a pure spirit that inspired the whole-hearted devotion of its worshippers.

Their attitude toward the government was likewise happy, on the whole, being very much that of a child toward a parent. English-speaking people generally have such a prejudice against paternalism that they are somewhat blind to its good side, its human quality. The government of New France was neither a vague abstraction nor an impersonal machine. It had a heart as well as an intelligence, and was like a wise father who knows how to humor his children. The principal agent of the government in each locality was the captain of militia. With few exceptions, there was only one in each parish, and he was never of seigniorial rank. He was usually the most responsible and respected habitant of the community. Legally he received his powers from above; practically he derived his authority from below. Though he secured his commission from the governor, he really owed his appointment to the people, for they were regularly consulted and their approval was considered necessary. This informal election, generally held at the church after the Sunday service, seems to have resulted in the selection of a truer representation than do most of our formal elections. An honored seat in the church, a larger piece of holy bread than the other habitants received at the celebration of the Mass, the right to wear a sword, an occasional gift of powder and shot from the governor, and the great respect of his fellows, constituted his only rewards. The laws and orders of the government he read out to the people at the church door on Sundays, and none could plead ignorance, for they all attended divine service regularly. Coming through him, the commands of government were commonly obeyed; but if they were not, he reported to the governor or the intendant, who, after careful investigation, might impose a fine upon the delinquent.

The habitants' regard for the government was also fostered by the administration of justice. Every criminal accusation was made privately to the *procureur du roi*, or king's attorney, who thereupon secretly explored the case to discover if there was sufficient evidence to warrant a trial; and unless he concluded that there was, the accused was never apprehended and might not even know that he had been under a cloud. Such a method protected the innocent without shielding the guilty, as it might have done had the colony been larger. The courts were numerous and sat twice a week. Indeed, justice was so speedy, so cheap, and so sound that men sought rather than avoided the courts, and litigation might almost be said to have been a favorite pastime.

As a people, the Canadians were then, as now, noted for their sprightly and lively character. A British officer who came to Quebec in 1768 observed that "the peasantry salute and bow to one another with as good an air as people of higher rank; they testify no bashfulness nor awkwardness in any company of what rank so ever, but speak and act with great ease and freedom. This indeed they are taught and habituated to from the moment they begin to crawl about, and, by the time they are fourteen years of age, possess it as much as their parents. . . . Their vivacity they inherit from their European ancestors, to which the climate they live in, and their manner of feeding more upon vegetable than animal substances, may contribute." They were not given to strong drink, but the men, he added, "are much addicted to smoking tobacco, which they are accustomed to from mere boys." In common with many other English-speaking people of that time, he condemned them as lazy. But this accusation is easily explained away. Their wants were no greater than their needs, and nature was bountiful. Moreover, they possessed that enviable genius, an infinite capacity for enjoying life. At work and play they sang and laughed. Every Sunday and every saint's day the parish church drew them to religious duties and social pleasures. The long winter months were never dreary but were always filled with good cheer. The river valley rang with the joy of young and old, skating, horseracing, or driving carioles, for they had horses in plenty. Indoors there was an endless round of festivity. Cards were a thief of time, and dancing feet sped away the hours. Around the stove, tongues wagged in gossip and related stories that made sides rock or hair stand on end. The folk songs and folklore of old French Canada are eloquent testimony that no children of the earth ever had a gayer or more wholesome existence.

Such was the normal life of the great majority of the Canadians. Only a small minority dwelt in the towns. Of these there were only two, for Three Rivers was but a straggling village of hardly a hundred houses. Montreal was surrounded by a wall and a ditch, but was counted a place of no strength. It was less than a mile long, running from the present McGill Street to Cartier Square. At its widest it was only three hundred and fifty yards across. Along the north ran the creek, which has since disappeared under Craig Street; on the south the town was bounded by the St. Lawrence and by St. Peter's River, over which Ste. Ann's Market was later built. There were only two thoroughfares traversing the town, the modern Notre Dame and St. Paul streets, and the former was interrupted by the old parish church on the Place d'Armes. The population, which may have been five thousand, had outgrown the walls to form the Quebec Suburb at the east end, the Récollet Suburb at the other extreme, and the St. Lawrence Suburb across Craig Street Creek along the road leading to Sault au Récollet. The General Hospital, which the Grey Nuns had taken over in 1755, also lay outside the walls, just south of the little St. Peter's River. As a reminder of the heavenly origin of the town, so charmingly related by Parkman, one-fifth of its area was occupied by the houses and gardens of various religious organizations, the Jesuits, the Sisters of the Congregation, the Seminary of St. Sulpice, and the Récollet friars. The rest of the town was built for the service of Mammon, Montreal being the capital of the North American fur trade, and the lay population was obviously infected by the devil-may-care spirit which that traffic has usually engendered. Some might adduce this as the cause of the frequent fires that had preyed upon the place and led to the substitution of stone structures for wooden buildings.

Quebec was a very different sort of place. It was a staid town, for it was far removed from the contagion of the fur trade and was the seat of the bishop, the capital of the colony, and the Gibraltar of America. Perched on the cliff, three hundred feet and more above the river, stood the bastion of Cape Diamond. This was the highest, the strongest, and the most southerly point of the triangular town enclosed on the north by the St. Charles, on the east by the St. Lawrence, and on the landward side by the line of fortifications, which ran north-northwest. Along the northern half of the eastern side of Quebec the cliff did not plunge right into the river. Here, just above the water level at high tide, was a little narrow shelf on which the dwellings, warehouses, and shops of the Lower Town lay huddled together. Trade had not yet contaminated the proud Upper Town, which belonged wholly to God, the king, and a few gentry. Here were the spacious college of the Jesuits, the seminary that Laval had founded, the Hôtel Dieu, the houses of the Récollets and the Ursulines, and two other convents, the parish church, which served also as a cathedral, the Bishop's Palace, and, just across the way, the Castle of St. Louis, the abode of the governor. On the northwest corner, just outside the walls, was the suburb of St. Roch. To the east of this stood the Intendant's Palace, and three-quarters of a mile to the west, on the southern bend of the St. Charles, lay the General Hospital.

In further contrast to Montreal, which had been surrendered whole, without a blow, Quebec was a town of ruins, so badly had it been battered by the British guns. Lying off by itself, the General Hospital was mercifully preserved unscathed, but not a building in the town had escaped the deadly work of shot and shell. The bare walls were all that was left standing of the parish church. One-third of the houses were completely destroyed, and many more were so shattered that they had to be pulled down. The streets were cumbered with fallen beams and piled with broken masonry. In 1754 the population had been computed at eight thousand, but no more than thirty-five hundred were recorded by the census taken shortly after the conquest. Truly it was a stricken city.

The blight of war had also hit the countryside. Around and below Quebec many a charred heap marked the site of a once happy cottage, for the invaders had been driven to use the sternest methods to prevent the habitants from taking up arms against them or bearing succor to the beleaguered garrison. And throughout the colony the people were more or less exhausted by the protracted strife. The whole community was suffering from economic pleurisy, for the ever-growing volume of paper currency had long since driven all sound money out of circulation. The merchants had been forced to part with their wares and the habitants to yield their flour and grain, their horses and cattle, in return for the notes of a bankrupt government. The government which had thus impoverished them had also worn them out in countless corvées and endless militia service, until they could stand the strain no longer. All these sacrifices had been in vain, and as the final crisis was clearly approaching, with the British closing in on Montreal, the habitants had deserted the hopeless struggle, thereby precipitating the fall of their country.

The fall of Quebec on September 18, 1759, though it sealed the doom of

Canada, was only the surrender of one fortified place. The articles that the British Admiral Saunders and General Townshend and the French commander De Ramezay signed on that day were, therefore, short and few, only eleven in all. The members of the garrison were allowed to "march out with their arms and baggage, drums beating, matches lighted, with two pieces of French cannon, and twelve rounds for each piece," and were to be "embarked as conveniently as possible, to be sent to the first port in France." The rest of the artillery and military stores were yielded up with the town. Before the delivery of the gate the British had to post soldiers to safeguard "the churches, convents, and principal habitations." Upon laying down their arms the residents were guaranteed the possession of their private property, and until their future condition should be settled by a treaty of peace, they were not to be removed nor even obliged to quit their houses, for neither side wished a repetition of the Acadian tragedy. Moreover, article six stated that until a treaty was negotiated "the free exercise of the Roman religion is granted, likewise safeguards to all religious persons, as well as to the bishop," who had retired to Montreal. He was to be allowed "to come and exercise, freely and with decency, the functions of his office, whenever he shall think proper."

The document that Vaudreuil, the Canadian governor, and Jeffrey Amherst, the British commander-in-chief, signed on September 8, 1760, is commonly called the Capitulation of Montreal, but it should be known as the Capitulation of Canada. Because it involved very much more, it has five times as many articles and is eight times as long as the Capitulation of Quebec. The military provisions, which were most explicit, occupy the forefront of the document. Denied the honors of war, all troops whether in Montreal or elsewhere were to lay down their arms, to be transported to France free of charge, and to take no more part in the war. Similarly, the governor and the intendant, with their staffs of officials, were to be carried home. Nor was any obstacle to be placed in the way of private individuals who wished to retire to France. All, whether civil or military, were to be allowed to carry with them their families and effects. They were also permitted to carry off their official papers, except charts and plans of the country and such archives as might be necessary for the government of the colony. But Vaudreuil demanded and Amherst promised that the registers of the supreme council of Quebec and all other documents belonging to that and other offices, including seigniorial and notarial records, "that may serve to prove the estates and fortunes of the citizens," should remain where they were. All property except that belonging to the government, which of course was surrendered, was to be left untouched in the hands of its owners, who were given full liberty to sell it and take away the produce "in bills of exchange, furs, specie, or other returns." No Canadian was to be molested in any way, but Amherst would not agree to extend any guarantee to the few Acadians who had come to the country. Inspired by the sad history of these people, Vaudreuil also tried to extract a promise that the Canadians who remained in the country should never be required to bear arms against France or her allies. Amherst, however, insisted that they become the subjects of the British king. There had been too many half-subjects down in Acadia. Nor would he give any more explicit answer to Vaudreuil's demand that the old laws be preserved by the new government.

So much has been made of the provisions touching religion that it is necessary to examine them closely. Article twenty-seven reads in part as follows: "The free exercise of the Catholic, Apostolic, and Roman religion, shall subsist entire, in such manner that all the states and the people of the towns and countries, places and distant posts, shall continue to assemble in the churches, and to frequent the sacraments as heretofore, without being molested in any manner, directly or indirectly." Amherst agreed to this wide stipulation, but to the further demand that the new government continue the legal obligation of the tithe he replied that this "will depend upon the king's pleasure." The secular clergy were to retain all their rights and functions. The communities of nuns were to remain inviolate in all their privileges, but Amherst withheld a similar promise from the Jesuits, the Récollets, and the Sulpicians "till the king's pleasure be known." They were, however, guaranteed their property. Even the Indians were to be included in this covenant of religious liberty and were to retain their missionaries.

But however large were the promises of the British, there was one thing that threatened to undermine them all. There was no bishop in the land, for Pontbriand, whose functions had been guaranteed in the capitulation of Quebec, had died on May 8, just four months before Montreal was surrendered. Without a bishop no priest could be ordained, and death might slowly rob the people of their clergy and their religion. If the British promises were to mean anything, there must be a succession of priests, and for this there must be a bishop. The great question was how to get him. Though invested by the pope, he

had been nominated by the king. This method had been possible as long as Canada belonged to France, but it became impossible the moment the country was transferred to Britain. A Roman Catholic king might pick a Roman Catholic bishop, but a Protestant king certainly could not. Vaudreuil suggested therefore that the French monarch retain his right to nominate to the see of Quebec. Of course there were also political motives behind the proposal, and they must have leaped to Amherst's eye. By imposing his veto he left the great question unsolved.

Only comfortable critics at Versailles could condemn the surrender of the country upon these terms. They were just and generous, and do equal honor to the Canadian governor and the British commander. Vaudreuil demanded everything that was essential to the honor of the troops and the welfare of the people, and Amherst denied nothing that he could possibly have granted, except the honors of war to the garrison. This exception was but a detail of the moment. The only thing that really mattered in the transaction signed on September 8, 1760, was the transfer of a country and its people from one empire to another for a period at least and possibly for all time.

Many tears have been shed over these foundlings on the banks of the St. Lawrence, exhausted materially and physically by a bankrupt government and a vain war, deserted by an unnatural and extravagant mother, and endangered spiritually by falling under the yoke of an alien and heretical government. Even heaven seemed to have betrayed them in their hour of trial by stealing away their bishop. This pitiful picture of these people in 1760 is of more than ephemeral interest. It is one of the most important and abiding things in Canadian history, for the glorious contrast presented by the condition of their children in successive generations has been and will continue to be the chief inspiration of the French Canadian race.

But the pathos of their plight on the morrow of the conquest must not be overdrawn. New France was already separated from Old France by more than the Atlantic. The country that gave birth to the colony was not the same country when she lost it, for she was sickening with the disease that was soon to shock the world. Nor had the colony stood still. Like the English colonies, it had been quietly drifting away from Europe and may even have drifted further, for immigration to Canada had ceased two generations before, whereas English recruits were still pouring into the colonies to the south. Thus cut off, and living under very different conditions from Frenchmen at home, the Canadians tended to become conscious that they were a distinct people. The historic antipathy between Montcalm and the Canadian-born Vaudreuil was tragic testimony to the growing estrangement. Although the final separation did not come in hate, there was a drop of bitterness in the cup whenever Canadians drank to the health of their lost mother, for had not France really abandoned them to their fate? This touch of resentment went far to neutralize the romantic feeling that the severance of the tie added to their filial affection.

The chief love of the Canadians was for Canada and not for France. The fortunes of war revealed this truth and the blessings of peace were to emphasize it. Never was a people more war-weary than were the Canadians in 1760. For generations they had been fighting, first redskins and then white men, until they could fight no more. Now, in a great revulsion from war, they reverted to type, as far as was possible in the New World, and struck ever deeper roots into the soil. Paradoxical as it may seem, they had been forced to live an unnatural life under governors of their own blood, but under rulers of an alien race they were to find themselves.

One other important factor in their situation at this time was long obscured by the legend of a social decapitation. It used to be said that the better classes as a whole retired to France after the conquest, leaving behind only a helpless and hopeless mass. This tradition was doubly false. In the first place, most of the so-called better classes clung to the colony. In the second place, these were not the real leaders of the people. Although the wealthier seigniorial families lent grace to the society of the towns, chiefly Quebec, and many of the noblesse had distinguished themselves in numerous campaigns and more numerous forays, the real leaders of the people were two classes of men who sprang from their own midst and remained in daily and intimate contact with them—the curés and the captains of militia. They were the true shepherds, and they never for one moment dreamed of deserting their flocks.

A. R. M. Lower, *Colony to Nation: a History of Canada,* (Toronto, 1946), pp. 63-64, 66-69. Reprinted by permission of Longmans Canada Ltd.

Conquered

At last the inevitable happened, French resistance collapsed and the people were left unprotected. The bitter agony of Canada had begun.

It is hard for people of English speech to understand the feelings of those who must pass under the yoke of conquest, for there is scarcely a memory of it in all their tradition. Conquest is a type of slavery and of that too they have no memory, except as masters. Conquest, like slavery, must be experienced to be understood.

But anyone can at least intellectually perceive what it means. The entire life-structure of the conquered is laid open to their masters. They become second-rate people. Wherever they turn, something meets their eyes to symbolize their subjection. It need not be the foreign military in force, it need not be the sight of the foreign flag, it may be some quite small matter: a common utensil of unaccustomed size and shape, let us say, taking the place of one familiar. And then there is the foreign speech, perhaps not heard often, but sometimes heard, and sometimes heard arrogantly from the lips of persons who leave no doubt that the conquered are, in their estimation, inferior beings. Even the kindness of the superior hurts. The educated may make their peace, learn the foreign language and find many areas in common, but the humble cannot cross the gulf: they feel pushed aside in their own homes. Hence it is that nationalism always lives longest, even if not blazing up into fierce flame, in the hearts of the people, who seek to maintain their own ways by the passiveness of their behaviour and little by little, as opportunity offers, edge forward into any chance space left vacant by their masters.

No one can suggest that the English conquest, as conquests go, was cruel or English government harsh. If the French in Canada had had a choice of conquerors, they could not have selected more happily than fate did for them. But conquerors are conquerors: they may make themselves hated or they may get themselves tolerated; they cannot, unless they abandon their own way of life and quickly assimilate themselves, in which case they cease to be conquerors, make themselves loved. As long as French are French and English are English, the memory of the Conquest and its effects will remain. Not until that great day comes when each shall have lost themselves in a common Canadianism will it be obliterated. . . .

. . . the problem was not merely 60,000 new subjects, for the conquered people formed a strong society in a geographical habitat of crucial importance. The problem, therefore, consisted in associating a new and very different kind of community with old ones which were nearly all of a piece. The English colonies were all self-governing and extremely sensitive about their rights. Could New

France be made over at once? If it were
not and if authoritarian government were
continued, would that not generate suspi-
cions and antagonisms towards the Imperial power? Here was an immediate
political dilemma.

Another and sharper problem was to
arise in time, as members of the two
societies met in the new province of Quebec. How were two such different families
to live in this one house? Was there a
point that they had in common? In addition to the differences in language, faith
and institutions there were many others,
stemming from the same root, equally in-
tractable. Once Canada became an English possession the profound antithesis
emerged, the vast conflict in philosophies,
which ever since has kept the country
divided and which, in presenting it with
a problem of such proportions, constitutes
the principal theme of Canadian history.

The French peasantry of the St.
Lawrence valley were a chip off the old
European block: they duplicated on North
American soil the pre-Reformation peasant society of the old world; they represented the very essence of the medieval,
rural, Catholic way of life. To the Catholic everywhere, especially to the rural
Catholic, life is more than livelihood. It
is a series of ritual acts such as being
born, becoming of age, marrying, beget-
ting, dying, each of which, properly performed, brings its satisfactions and its
reward. There is little need for striving,
little occasion for the notion of progress.
The rural life harmonizes well with this
conception: man is subject to nature and
to nature's moods; he learns to acquiesce
in the drought and the flood, the good
years and the bad. As his animals and
plants grow and come to harvest, so he
grows and comes to harvest, a creature
of nature and of nature's God. It is the
simplest and oldest of all religions, Catholic almost by accident.

Into this unchanging world, there
comes bursting the hurly-burly of the
English man of business. He has long
since cut his associations with the soil. He
is in a hurry. He wants to get things done.
He has ends to gain. He has an object in
life. That object is one comprehended
only remotely by the peasant. From the
first the new world had released in men
the passion of greed. Greed, as an ordinary human quality, the peasant can
understand well enough but not greed
erected into a way of life and fortified
both with the majesty of law and the
sanction of a religion. Yet no set of men
have so systematically set up acquisition
as an object in itself and made it the
centre of a cult, a new god Mammon, as
have the men of business of the English-
speaking world. In 1760, the new creed
had not gone as far as it has today; it has
almost swamped us now, especially in
the new world, but in 1760, the older elements in English life still resisted it like
feudalism in its 18th century form of
aristocracy and the more traditional elements in the Church of England. It was
in the fighting and governmental services
that these found their strongest expression. It was, therefore, these that were to
have the best relations with the conquered
Canadian Catholics. The weight of the
English thrust into the new province was
not, however, to consist in them but in
men representing that new way of life
which had already appropriated for itself
a theology by which its conduct was justified and rationalized.

The connection between Protestantism,
and the especially close connection between Calvinism, and material achievement has been the subject of much investigation. Wherever Calvinism has

prevailed, societies largely committed to the commercial and industrial way of life have arisen. The coincidence seems logical, for while the spirit of acquisition is as old as humanity, Calvinism subtly reinforces it. Its doctrine of 'the elect' has led directly to the attempt on the part of the individual to reassure himself that he is one of the elect: and what more visible sign of election unto salvation could God give him than by prospering him? In this and many other ways Calvinism accentuated the motives of action having to do with success and accomplishment. Everywhere it found its most congenial soil in urban areas, among the middle classes, and nowhere more so than in the New World. For there, in communities of English or Dutch origin, traditions that might have held the success motive in check were weak: most people had come to the New World to improve their lot and, with their middle class and Calvinistic background, improvement almost necessarily meant material improvement. There had logically developed an ethic quite unlike the older Catholic code, with different standards of value, despising the older ideal with all the intolerance that the new and the moving invariably shows for the old and the static. This ethic of material success passed over easily into success in terms of accomplishment or of power and in these forms afforded that driving energy which has mainly made America. In so doing it reduced most elements in society, such as for example, education, to its own utilitarian terms. And even life itself, for deep in the heart of Puritanism there is a denial of life. The dynamic of the commercial ethic has transformed the world but it has left little room for the things of the spirit, and where societies have been completely dominated by it, they have been societies of attenuated art and meagre culture, above all societies whose parsimoniousness with life has made them hollow at the centre.

If Canadian history is to be understood at all, it is necessary first of all to be able to understand and apply to common situations these two ways of life: the static Catholic-rural, careless of well-being, not over-burdened with social responsibility, prodigal of life, welcoming many children, not grieving too intensely if many die and others live mis-shapen; and the dynamic Calvinist-commercial with its devotion to acquisition and its haunting fear of animal 'robustiousness'. They touch every corner of the national structure and there is not a person living or who has lived in Canada who has not been affected by the antithesis between them, for it has determined the very essence of the country's politics, religion and society. It is not a simple task to reveal it, as it should be revealed, on every page and in every incident.

Close analysis of the antithesis between commercialism and agrarianism pushes it beyond race and religion. There lurks in it some basic contrast in the attitude towards life. On one hand stand those who are close to the soil, irrevocably committed to the land in which and by which they live; and on the other those who simply regard Mother Earth as a source of good things, who cut down its forests and tear out its minerals regardless of its future and then, if opportunity offers, rush off to pleasanter places. This selfish and hostile attitude towards the earth by which man lives gives one pole of modern history: the driving, ambitious, accomplishing, mechanistic pole. It gives us the opportunists, the exploiters, the men with no past and little future. The other attitude gives the pole of acquiescence, acceptance, harmony with life. It produces the custodians of society, the fathers of the race. These attitudes, crystallized in the contrasting figures of the business man and the settler, but not confined to either, are writ large on every page of Canadian history and they, as well as their racial and religious manifestations, must be understood if Canadians are to understand themselves as a people and their country as a nation

Thomas Chapais, *Cours d'Histoire du Canada,* Tome 1, 1760-1791, (Montréal, Bernard Valiquette, n.d.), pp. 3-12, 29-30, 60. (Translated C.N.)

All Honour

to the Enemy

. . . Our Old Regime was finished, a new regime was beginning for us.

It opened under the most sombre auspices. Crushed by numbers, decimated and ruined by war, truncated by the fall of the government which had, till then, administered them, forcibly separated from the mother-country whose faith, language, traditions, manners, laws and customs had woven the web of their national existence, the Canadians saw themselves subjected to a foreign power whom they had learned to fear, and whose religion, idiom, usages and laws were so many menaces and objects for apprehension. Their situation was distressing and justified all alarms. An abyss had opened before their feet, henceforth separating their past from their future. During the three years that had elapsed between the capitulation of Montreal and the Treaty of Paris, they could still nourish the uncertain hope that Canada would be returned to France, as had happened in 1632. But the days of Richelieu had passed. The promulgation of the Treaty of Paris dealt a death blow to this great illusion. Their fate was sealed. They would no longer be French. . . . Separated, isolated, deprived of all means of communication with the mother-country forced by defeat to abandon them, they saw themselves reduced to their own resources, or, more correctly, to heart-rending weakness under the yoke of their completely and irrevocably victorious, century-long foe. What a sombre horizon for our fathers! . . . Could they save something from this great shipwreck of the French race in America? . . . Would there be a tomorrow for their nationality? The present was desolate and the future sinister.

Gentlemen, turning your eyes for a moment from this sad scene, would you leap forward the space of a century? We are in Quebec. The ancient capital of New France is rejoicing. A happy crowd rushes towards the historic site of the old episcopal palace erected by Mgr. de Saint-Vallier, where another building consecrated to the deliberations of an autonomous legislature stands. To the noise of cannons and popular acclaim, a governor, representing the British Crown, has just opened the first session of the representative body now charged with enacting our civil laws, our education system, our public domain, and our national institutions. And this governor, escorted by English troops who present arms to him as to a sovereign, surrounded by English officers who form a guard of honour, is a man of the French race and language who has just presided at the inauguration of a French legislature, created by an act of the Parliament of England, freely to administer the French province formed from all the territory that once comprised the core of the ancient New France.

Is there not a striking contrast, gentlemen, between these two scenes!

Who could have foreseen in 1763 that the descendants of a conquered people could have participated, in 1867, in as triumphal a scene as that which we have just described? Who would have dared to predict so glorious a survival at the time of defeat, isolation and national collapse? Before such a historical phenomenon, he who is interested in proceeding from effects to causes naturally asks himself by what means did the prodigious revival take place, in what way was this victorious evolution accomplished, what were its stages, and how could our nationality, apparently wounded to death in 1760, heal its wounds, recover a new vitality, and win not only its right to exist, but its right to freedom? . . .

First of all, a question forces itself on our attention. What was the most dangerous trial of the cataclysm of 1760 for our fathers? Was it the loss of the political institutions under which they had lived till then? One might be tempted to believe so; but nothing would be more false . . .

What appeared as the most redoubtable peril to our fathers at the beginning of the English domination was the anguishing uncertainty of their religious situation and of the legal system to which they would be subjected. . . . Those whom victory had made their rulers appeared to go out of their way to reassure the Canadians by wise and conciliatory measures. From the fall of 1760 to the summer of 1764, that is to say from the capitulation of Montreal to the publication of the commission which appointed Murray as Governor-General, there existed a *de facto* government obviously destined to be replaced by a more regularly organized one at the conclusion of the peace. . . .

As can be seen, this temporary administration, hastily instituted after the

Conquest, did not appear to have been inspired by a desire to ostracise or oppress. But let us observe here how words often change the realities. The military element played a large rôle in this regime. And, from this fact, people have been led to call it a "Military Regime." This title has been fatal. To a great many, "Military Regime" means the rule of the sword and iniquitous arbitrariness. Several of our writers have let themselves be misled by it. . . .

We are at the beginning of the English domination. We want to know whether the French Canadian nation will survive the Conquest and the collapse of the Old Regime. Under the perilous conditions in which events had placed our people in 1764, no doubt the religious question was important, but was it a pre-eminent one, and ought it to be placed in the forefront of our studious inquiries? In other words, was its national importance great enough for us to assign it such primacy? . . . Yes, the religious question was one of capital importance, of vital importance for our nationality in 1764. And a very simple observation will suffice to prove it. Two powers had co-operated at the birth and in the growth of the French Canadian nationality—France and the Church. France had disappeared forever in the storm of 1760. But the Church had remained. . . .

Yes, if our Church survived the torment of 1763 and the years that followed without sinking, we owe it to him [Briand], to his firmness, his loyalty, his prudence, and to his coolness. All honour to his pure and noble memory! Honour too to his devoted collaborators, . . . And why should we not add?—justice is the supreme law of history—honour to those enlightened Englishmen, those officials and British statesmen, Murray, Cramahé, Carleton, Burke, Rockingham, who, by their sense of justice and by their policy, decided to second the efforts of our leaders . . .

Michel Brunet, "Premières réactions des vaincus de 1760 devant leurs vainqueurs", *La Présence Anglaise et les Canadiens,* (Montréal, Beauchemin, 1958), pp. 37–48. (Translated C.N.) Printed by permission of the author.

The First Reactions

of the Conquered

All historians have emphasized the very cordial relations that were established between the *Canadiens* and their conquerors from the first months of the English occupation. The fact remains undeniable. We will never know exactly what the people thought within themselves, but their outward attitudes manifested complete submission.

The haste of the conquered to submit to the authority of a century-old enemy, their docility, the servility of their ruling classes surprises a twentieth-century observer a little. The latter has been the witness of the courageous resistance of the countries occupied by the Germans during the course of the last war. The words "collaboration" and "collaborators" have a very bad press in our day. Our contemporary history textbooks have taught us to admire the desperate struggles of minorities—Greeks, Belgians, Poles, Italians, Hungarians—subjected to foreign domination. One must realize that the conduct of the *Cana-*

diens during the first years of the English occupation has never inspired, nor ever will inspire, poets to search for acts of collective heroism.

How can the almost spontaneous submission of the conquered in 1760 be explained? The historian A. L. Burt claims that the benevolence of the English soldiers, the completeness of their victory, the impossibility for the *Canadiens* to dream of vengeance, and the benefits to the country of the restoration of peace, all contributed to the solid and peaceful establishment of English domination in Canada . . . Mr. Burt's explanation does not take sufficient account of the conquered themselves. The same reproach might be made against the explanations given by most of the other historians.

No one has thus far attempted to write the history of this "moral conquest." Far more serious than the military conquest of which it was only the consequence, it completely modified the historical development of the people France had established on the banks of the St. Lawrence. Begun in 1760, this "moral conquest" has continued since that time. To retrace its stages is to describe how a conquered people loses the privilege of normal development. Mr. Burt, and all those who have used the expression "moral conquest", have never paused to evaluate its terrible meaning. . . .

The conquered *Canadiens* expected worse. The struggle had been long and without mercy. Official propaganda had never ceased repeating to them that the English conqueror would be pitiless . . .

The enemy himself had not been sparing with his threats . . . As for Murray, he showed the inhabitants of the Islands of Sorel and its vicinity that he, too, practised the art of total war.

The conduct of the French officers and of the metropolitan authorities made the conquered even more unhappy. On the fifteenth of June, 1760, Vaudreuil and Bigot announced to them that the government was suspending payment on letters of exchange. English propaganda hastened to explain to the *Canadiens* that they were the victims of a truly royal bankruptcy . . .

From 1759 to 1760 the *Canadiens* lived through a year of veritable nightmare. The conqueror had before him a conquered and prostrated people.

The British knew how to make use of the circumstances. The prostrate condition of the conquered served the ends of the conquerors admirably. They played a magnanimous rôle by being generous and sympathetic. No sooner was Murray in Quebec than he explained to his superior the multiple advantages of a policy of mercy. Paternalistic and protective, he calmed the fears of a population that was totally resigned. . . .

The administration of justice suffered no radical change. In this area as in others, the military authorities proceeded with prudence and wisdom. The *Canadiens* could but be pleased with the situation. Their fears and the gloomy prophecies of the French propaganda had not materialized. . . .

The generosity of the conqueror, his benevolence, his solicitude for the general interest, and his spirit of justice gained him the hearts of the conquered. The latter had only to draw a parallel between the conduct of the English and that of the former governors of the country. The comparison, unfortunately, was not to the advantage of the latter . . .

The *mandements* of the clergy and the petitions of the inhabitants on the occasion of the ratification of the peace treaty are very revealing.

The grand vicar of Three Rivers believed that "the peace is made, My Very Dear Brothers, for the well-being of humanity." He foresaw that Canada "would forever remain to the glorious victor George III, King of Great Britain." A eulogy of the sovereign and an appeal to the gratitude, fidelity, and "perfect submission" that all his *Canadien* subjects owed him, complete the document. M. Perrault even affirms that religion depends on "this fidelity" and this "perfect submission."

Regarding the history of the military regime, M. Briand observes that its mildness indicated God's mercy to the conquered. Under the new government, the people will taste "the sweetness of a happy and durable peace." The vicar-general insists on loyalty to the monarchy: "Be correct in the fulfilment of the duties of loyal subjects attached to their princes; and you will have the consolation of finding a king who is good-natured, benevolent, and diligent to make you happy, and favourable to your religion . . . There is nothing that can exempt you from perfect obedience, scrupulous and exact fidelity, and an inviolable and sincere attachment to your new Monarch and to the interests of the nation to which we have just been joined. . . . "

Should the general attitude and the reactions of the principal spokesman of the population surprise us? A few *Canadiens*, who might be judged guilty of unconscionable attitudes, even give the impression of rejoicing at the "change of masters. . . . " It would have been difficult for the conquerors to find a conquered group better disposed.

The generation of 1760 lived in the period of enlightened despotism. These men and women of the *ancien régime* recognized only one political system: the absolute monarchy. They accepted it quite naturally, without discussion. The French and American Revolutions had not yet preached the rights of peoples to rule themselves. Liberal and democratic nationalism did not yet exist. Monarchists to their very souls, used to living in a strongly hierarchical society, attached to their corner of land, the *Canadiens* submitted without reservation to the authority of the new monarch that the destiny of arms had given them. Their most lucid leaders had left the conquered colony or were preparing to do so. The leading classes that remained in the country imagined that they would preserve complete freedom of action. Could the *Canadiens* have foreseen that the Conquest would fatally and radically modify their historical evolution as a distinct entity in North America? They realized that they comprised the immense majority of the colonial population. Naturally enough, they held the illusion that they would always remain so. Several English governors did not think otherwise. Even "joined" to a strange nation and members of a new empire, they were convinced Canada would continue to belong to them. They believed themselves to be wholly secure under the tutelage of a king who was "good-natured, benevolent, and diligent to make you happy." Under these conditions why should they be worried?

For the Canadians of 1760, the Conquest was no more than a simple change in the succession to the throne. Six generations later, some of their descendants still share this same *naiveté*. Louis XV had abandoned the colony. The old king was dead. The new subjects of His Britannic Majesty showed themselves prepared to call out submissively and in chorus, "Long live King George!"

Marjorie G. Reid, "Pitt's Decision to Keep Canada in 1761", *Canadian Historical Association Report*, 1926, pp. 21–27. Reprinted by permission of the Canadian Historical Association.

Canada, Yes,

Guadaloupe, No

The decision of British statesmen to keep Canada after the Seven Years' War has never been fully explained. . . . If Quebec had not been conquered in 1759, Great Britain could not have won it by diplomacy in 1763. The ministers of Louis XV would not have surrendered without a struggle the colony which their predecessors had fondly named *La Nouvelle France*. . . . Great Britain was obliged to surrender some of her conquests. Why did she keep Canada? . . .

. . . When diplomatic negotiations formally began, in the spring of 1761, Pitt gave to his ambassador, Hans Stanley, no definite instructions about the British terms except that the basis of negotiation should be the *uti possidetis*. The young diplomat was warned against being drawn unwittingly into any preliminary statement of terms. France, said Pitt, had been the aggressor and the loser, and it was for her to offer concessions. When Stanley reached Paris he reported that the French foreign minister, the Duke of Choiseul, had endeavoured by "cheerful

dinners in the highest company" and by every art of conversation, to discover the intentions of the British ministry, especially in regard to Canada and Guadeloupe. Stanley was on his guard, and the onus of making the first propositions fell upon the French. They were briefly set forth in a paper which is referred to in the British correspondence as the "Little Leaf" of June 17.

The proposals of the Duke of Choiseul to Mr. Stanley: He demands the restitution of Guadeloupe and Mariegalante, as well as of Goree, in exchange for the Island of Minorca: he proposes the absolute cession of Canada with the exception of Isle Royal, where no fortifications shall be built, and to confirm this cession France insists upon the preservation of the cod-fishery as it was established by the Treaty of Utrecht, and upon a definition of the boundaries of Canada in the region of the Ohio. . . .

Pitt replied to this "breaking of Choiseul's mind" by an informal counter-memorandum on June 26. In it he accepted the session of Canada, but objected to the limitations which had been coupled with it. Canada must be ceded "whole and entire, not mutilated or dismembered. . . . " The negotiations broke off in October, 1761, when Pitt resigned from his office over the dispute about the war with Spain. They were resumed by Bute late in the same year through informal agents, and brought to a conclusion in February, 1763. The cession of Canada was accepted by both parties at the beginning of these later discussions. During the debate in the House of Commons upon the preliminary terms of Bute's peace, Pitt commented once upon the surrender of Canada: "Of the dereliction of North America by the French, he entirely approved. But the negotiators had no trouble in obtaining this acquisition. It had been the *uti possidetis* in his own negotiation, to which the French had readily consented."

In Pitt's correspondence with the Colonial Governors, and with the military and naval officers in America, he had never indicated a definite intention of keeping Canada. There is, however, ample evidence that he was deeply concerned about the security of the American Colonies. In 1756 his reason for taking the offensive against the French was "the danger to which North America stands exposed." Two years later he aimed at securing the undisputed possession of the Ohio valley. In 1759, in the midst of the peace conversations instigated by the King of Prussia, he warned Amherst not to allow rumours of approaching peace to impede the military activities. He was determined in January, 1760 that nothing should "jeopardize the completion of the conquest of Canada." In June, reports of the French counter-attack upon Quebec led him to fear a "fatal catastrophe" there. It is clear that he wished to conquer New France, but whether he intended to keep it, or to exchange it for some other position, is not revealed. He regarded the security of the Atlantic colonies as a primary object of the war, but he nowhere stated definitely to officials in America that he considered the entire exclusion of the French as essential to that end. All through the year 1759, while the British forces were converging upon Quebec, Pitt was unwilling to commit himself about the terms of peace. During a debate in the Commons on Louisbourg, Pitt had replied to a question by Sir John Philipps and Alderman Beckford by saying that it was too early yet to decide what we would or would not restore. . . .

He was waiting until the end of the year's campaigns in America. On October 12 Knyphausen reported to Newcastle a conversation with Pitt: "He told me that, by what he could learn, Mr. Pitt did not think of keeping Louisbourg: but whether he would demolish it, or not, before it was given up, he did not know: he also thought Mr. Pitt had no notion of keeping Quebec, but that we should keep masters of the Lakes, Crown Point, Niagara, etc." A line through the Great Lakes was at that time being generally discussed in London. . . . The Earls of Newcastle and Hardwicke supported the idea. They favoured conciliatory terms, in order speedily to terminate the war. "If you keep Quebec," wrote Hardwicke to Newcastle, "you must keep all Canada, and Louisbourg as the key to it, and is that possible without fighting on forever?" One person of consequence, however, was not satisfied with the proposed restitutions in America—George II. On October 15 Newcastle reports to Hardwicke, "His Majesty then exclaimed against the restitutions in America, and, I hear, told the secretaries this day that Quebec must not be given up—we should never be safe there, if it was."

On the following day news arrived that Quebec had been surrendered to the British forces. Newcastle was thrown into a state of perturbation at the thought of reaching a decision about its future. Anticipations of difficulty of finding revenue for another year of war inclined him still to peace. The recent victories had, however, raised the spirits of the populace; they were inflamed by the hope of further victories if the war should continue. The attitude of Pitt was dubious. Holdernesse, the other secretary of state, was a mere cipher, "Pitt's footman," and the King was opposed to concessions. "I shall have a fine work upon my hands," wrote New-castle to Hardwicke, half suspecting his own ineffectiveness, "if I was to attempt settling ideas, and opinions, with the two present secretaries of state: especially informed as I am, or suspecting as I do, what is His Majesty's opinion as to peace, in general, and the particular terms of it." The Earl replied with a candour only equalled by his courtesy, "Besides the King and your Grace there is but one man material in this consideration, and that is Mr. Pitt: and, in the present situa-tion, whatever he will espouse and sup-port will probably go down with the populace." Pitt still reserved his judg-ment, although he deplored the extrava-gance of the King's demands, suspecting that they were made in order later to purchase concessions from the French in Germany. Pitt was at this time trying to maintain friendly relations with the two minor Bourbon powers, Spain and Naples, and he knew that they would re-sent excessive demands upon France, especially if these should disturb the equi-librium of power in America. In writing to Hardwicke about the news from Que-bec, Pitt tempered his satisfaction with an uneasy reference to the difficulty of draw-ing up such a peace as would please everybody. On the following day he ad-mitted to Newcastle that the King talked unreasonably about peace. On October 31 he discussed the terms of peace more frankly with Newcastle who, as usual, reported the conversation to Hardwicke:—

I mentioned to your Lordship, that Mr. Pitt had much ridiculed the King's way of talking about the conditions of peace, and the retaining *all our conquests*. He seem'd really desirous of peace, this winter, and upon reasonable terms—saw the difficulties of carrying on the war in Germany, for want of men—was desirous to keep Senegal,

and Gorée—seem'd more indifferent about *Guadaloupe*,—supposed, we must have Minorca again, and by his manner of dis-course, I should think by keeping possession of Niagara, the Lakes, Crown Point, and a proper security for our own colonies, the Bay of Fundy, etc., was all that he had at present determined. That, as to Quebec, Montreal, and even Louisbourg, they were points to be treated upon—not to be given up for nothing: but what might deserve consideration and be proper matter of negotiation.

In February, 1760, news came through the Prussian ambassador that France was willing to surrender Canada. Sir Andrew Mitchell, the British Ambassador at Berlin, corroborated the report in a "most secret" letter to Holdernesse: "He [Frederick] seems however to believe that France wishes for peace, and he added, that by the information he had from that country, they would be willing to purchase it with the loss of Canada." Frederick was at this time working for a general pacification. His wish may have been father to his report, for the French officially denied having made any such proposition. Fred-erick's suggestion was probably based upon a sentence from a letter written at this time by Choiseul to Voltaire, and for-warded by the latter to Frederick. The private correspondence of Choiseul and Voltaire was a regular channel for un-official communications with the King of Prussia. "Let him [Frederick] know," wrote Choiseul, "that in spite of our losses and as a result of his own losses, although the King may lose for a time his possessions in America, he is still able, if he so wishes, to annihilate the power of Prussia." Choiseul was probably recon-ciled to the loss of Canada—he had never shown much interest in northern colonies —but he was not yet ready to make an official proposal.

The accession of George III brought nearer the chances of peace, because he was not, like George II, anxious to prolong the war in order to win territory in Germany. During the summer of 1760, while success was coming to British arms abroad, he opposed all suggestions of peace. . . .

This state of uncertainty was not broken until early in April, 1761, when Newcastle heard, through a friend upon whom he could "absolutely depend," that France was willing to surrender Canada. By the middle of the month Pitt had communicated his final decision to the King and the Ministers:—

Mr. Pitt said, he had laid his thoughts fully before the King . . . that he thought the total destruction of the French in the East Indies, the probability of taking Martinico, and the effect that this expedition on Belisle might have, as well as the probable events of this campaign, would enable us to get a peace, which should secure to us, all Canada, Cape Breton, the Islands, the Harbours, the fisherys and particularly the exclusive fishery of Newfoundland. That if he was ever capable to sign a treaty without it he should be sorry, that he had ever got again the use of his right hand.

Pitt's decision to retain Canada was practically a final settlement of the question. His popularity was at its height, the machinations of George III to oust from the cabinet the only man strong enough to oppose a "patriot king," though begun in January, 1761, had not perceptibly weakened Pitt's influence. He was strong enough first to keep the cabinet and the foreign diplomats waiting for a year and a half while he made up his mind about the future of Canada, and then to settle the whole question in one brief interview with the king.

The long period of hesitation is an interesting commentary both upon the quality of Pitt's statecraft and upon the prevalent opinion as to the value of Canada. Pitt's strength was never the so-called strength of the obstinate man who determines upon a certain object and grimly fights until he obtains it. His decisions were final, at least when they concerned matters of critical importance, but he arrived at them without undue haste. The value of Canada was at that time uncertain. It must never again, he knew, become a base of attack upon the thirteen colonies, but perhaps that evil could be prevented and the broader interests of the nation better served by defining accurately the boundary between the two powers in America. In the spring of 1761 almost nothing was known in England about the economic possibilities of Canada. Two or three years later this ignorance had been partially dispelled by the reports of military officers stationed in the newly conquered territory, and by the letters of merchants who were beginning to exploit its resources. Both among Pitt's private papers, and in the pamphlets there is evidence that by 1763 opinion about Canada was changing. But in 1761 the only commercial argument in its favour was brought forward by the more advanced economists who wished to widen the American market. It was not, however, obviously necessary to give the colonists a whole continent before they could go in and possess it: their immediate hinterland might satisfy their present needs and the ambitions of the English manufacturers. The case for retaining Canada was by no means clear on these grounds. Pitt's hesitation seems to have come near to causing the loss of Canada in the winter of 1759–60, when his Prussian ally was urging peace, and the strain of the war was taxing the British treasury. At this juncture the stubbornness of George II may have prevented an offer to treat about the restoration of Canada. Canada owed much to the Hanoverians in these dubious early years of her history. She owed the Quebec Act in great measure to the determination of George III: it is possible that she owed her status as a member of the British Commonwealth to the German tenacity of George II.

The new elements which brought Pitt to his sudden decision of April, 1761, were, without doubt, the military and naval victories of 1760, and the unsolicited offer by France to cede Canada. Newcastle's timidity, though comprehensible, was not justified. Britain had found the resources for another year of war, and, moreover, she had every prospect of making further conquests in the campaigns which were just beginning. Pitt could not, however, keep all his conquests: he would probably have to choose between Canada and Guadeloupe. When he outlined the two alternatives in a confidential interview with the Prussian ambassador in December, 1760, he realized that one or other of these conquests must be given up, and in his earliest reply to Choiseul's proposals the surrender of Guadeloupe was foreshadowed. At the crucial moment the choice between Canada and Guadeloupe seems to have been precipitated by the court of France. Choiseul's first unofficial suggestion to the King of Prussia that France might have to surrender her possessions in America was corroborated in April, 1761. Immediately afterwards Pitt communicated his decision to the king. The choice of France was accepted, and the future of Canada was settled. It is significant in this connection that France did not at any future time attempt to recover Canada. During the Revolutionary War, Lafayette had a romantic notion of restoring the French Empire in America, but we have indisputable evidence that he was not supported by the French minister in that intention. Vergennes had been educated in the school of Choiseul. Neither of them thought that France's greatness depended upon the possession of colonies in the northern hemisphere. In the eighteenth century only a great manufacturing and trading nation could afford to maintain such colonies, for only to such a people had they a commercial value. By her decision of 1761 Britain attached to her empire a colony that had been left derelict (the word is almost justified) by France. Its future development was due partly to its great, unsuspected resources, partly to British enterprise, and partly to the breaking up of the first Empire. The first decision to retain it in 1761 seems, like many momentous choices, to have been reached almost by chance, yet destiny was already revealing itself in the reasons which brought about the decision. Pitt's policy was in keeping with the destiny of Great Britain. He had determined to make the American colonies safe, for he thought that they were necessary to the greatness of his country, and by conquering and keeping Canada for them he assured Britain of a second chance to build up a colonial empire. Like the more progressive economists of his day he valued continental colonies in the temperate zone because they provided markets for British manufactured goods: what was this opinion but an evidence of the industrial revolution of which Britain was the first to take advantage? France, on the other hand, was not anxious to keep Canada. Her greatness was on the continent of Europe. Choiseul's choice, like Pitt's, was in keeping with the destiny of his nation. . . .

Stanley Ryerson, *The Founding of Canada, Beginnings to 1815*, (Toronto, 1960), pp. 199–206. Reprinted by permission of Progress Books.

The Inestimable Benefits

of the Conquest

The transfer of Canada from the French colonial empire to the British posed a number of problems.

In the first place: What was to become of the Canadians themselves? Would there be an attempt to "make them over" into English-speaking Protestants? Would they suffer the same fate as the Acadians? (A remark of Gen. Murray's shows this was not excluded from consideration.)

Furthermore: What political and social changes would be engendered by the replacement of France's feudal-absolutist rule by that of a constitutional monarchy? The English bourgeois revolutions had resulted in the British colonies in America possessing parliamentary institutions in one form or another. What was to happen in the newly conquered colony?

It was widely claimed at the time that Britain had warred on France in order to spread what one contemporary described as "the inestimable benefits of political liberty and the Protestant religion." This idyllic view was stated afresh by Parkman with the resounding pronouncement that "England imposed by the sword on reluctant Canada the boon of rational and ordered liberty."

What "reluctant Canada" got was something a trifle different. It took her people thirty years of struggle to secure the right to an elective assembly; over seventy years (including a double-barreled uprising) to obtain a government answerable to parliament; and close to a century to get rid of the feudal burdens of seigneurial tenure (to say nothing of the privileged position of the Church in Quebec, which after two centuries is with us yet).

Is this to say that the change-over from French to British rule made no essential difference? Far from it. Three major changes resulted from the Conquest.

First: The existence in Britain of such democratic rights as were won in the 17th century English Revolution made it difficult for the authorities to refuse to their Canadian subjects (both "new" and "old") the right to assemble, petition and conduct political agitation: rights that had not existed in a like degree under the French régime, and which were exercised under the British with increasing vigor.

Second: Capitalist development in Britain (with the Industrial Revolution getting under way there) being much further ahead than was the case in France, the potentialities for economic and industrial growth in the colony were enhanced: as the example of the Atlantic colonies clearly showed. (At the same time, as this example also indicated, capitalist growth in the colony had to assert itself against the restrictive efforts of the imperial metropolis.)

Third: The British Conquest created a new *national* question in Canada. European rule over the aboriginal peoples was the first such problem; now there was added the domination of one European nationality over another. The French Canadians had come under British rule: what would become of this national community, so firmly rooted in the St. Lawrence valley?

The answer to this question was to be affected profoundly by another: that of the relations between the Empire and the Atlantic colonies, which now were heading towards a decisive struggle for their rights and ultimately for independence.

At Quebec, Gen. Murray mused over the fate of the newly-acquired colony: as a matter of policy, he wrote, it "should perhaps be destroyed; but there may be reasons why it should remain, as it is a guarantee for good behaviour of its neighbouring colonies. . . . "

. . . During this time, in the "Province of Quebec," the new relationships of British colonial rule were taking shape. From 1760–63 it was a régime of direct military occupation. The royal Proclamation of 1763 (following the Treaty of Paris) continued military rule in modified form with an appointed council assisting the governor. Freedom of trade, the matchless "blessing of British liberty," was proclaimed; but the representative institutions that were expected to accompany it were strangely absent. The Proclamation provided for an elective assembly: but none was forthcoming. Were the promises of "popular liberty," loudly proclaimed during the war with absolutist France, to prove nothing but a hoax? The few hundred English and colonial merchants who had moved into the province on the heels of the British armies were vociferous in their protests. . . .

Contrary to a widely-held opinion, most of the old ruling class stayed on after the Conquest. Those who went back to France were the small handful of top officials, including Bigot and his hangers-on. Of some two hundred seigneurs, about 140 remained in Canada. The change wrought by the Conquest was not a "social decapitation" due to an exodus of the seigneurs; it was, rather, the imposing of a new, Anglo-colonial ruling class on the conquered French Canadian nation.

The new rulers were at first made up in the main of the military and administrative officialdom; later on, their ranks were swelled by leading fur-traders and merchant-landowners.

The overriding concern of the British colonial authorities was to make Quebec a bulwark—and if need be a base of operations—against insubordination in the Atlantic colonies. To this end they decided to preserve feudalism and clerical privilege on the St. Lawrence: the best means, in Carleton's view, of securing for all time "a proper subordination of this province to Great Britain."

This policy of preserving intact the laws, customs and religious institutions of the Canadians meant in practice that their language was to be tolerated as well. The idea of any speedy anglicizing program had to be postponed.

Thus, on the one hand, the "new subjects" could thank the Atlantic colonists for the fact that the latter's rebellious pressure led London to make concessions to French Canadian national identity. On the other, they could blame the collaboration of seigneurs and clergy with the conquerors for the preservation of tithes and feudal burdens and absolutist rule, and the denial of democratic government.

As early as 1761, Murray was insisting on payment of seigneurial dues in hard cash. A few years later London decreed the granting of land on the basis of feudal tenure. For their part, the seigneurs strongly opposed the granting of elective institutions: the habitants, once given the vote, might get the upper hand in an Assembly! Already, there had been signs of popular opposition to the continuance of feudal imposition. At Chambly in 1762 it was reported "that several inhabitants of the place refuse to work on the king's road"—the hated *corvée* of enforced, unpaid labor. There were other incidents of refusal by habitants to carry out transport duties as demanded by the military. But the hatred of feudal oppression did no more than smoulder in the early years of the occupation; it flared up later, during the American Revolution.

Part II

The Military Regime: That Liberty Which is Greater Than English Liberty

The typical interpretative approach of Canadian historians to the period 1760 to 1763, of which A. L. Burt is an ideal example, has been neatly characterized by that historian in many pithy phrases. The above title is one of these; another is "Pity for the whole Canadian race", the dominant theme of Murray's policy, according to Burt. The kindness, the understanding of the occupying armies was long ago claimed by many contemporary witnesses, and by a long, long list of historians since that day. Burt keeps good company: Chapais, Lower, Sulte, McInnis, Wade, Groulx and the rest of the pantheon of Canadian historians. Yet Canada was a conquered country. Burt's selection emphasizes one aspect of the Military Regime; the "Proclamations of the Military Governors" presents a slightly different aspect of the period. In effect, martial law prevailed. That it was not more severe is due to the compliance of the conquered as much as to the benevolence of the conqueror.

François-Xavier Garneau, an exception to the usual historical interpretation, angrily calls the period a tyranny. His reason: the newly conquered *Canadiens*, not yet officially ceded to the British Crown, were not permitted the benefits of being *British subjects*, a droll criticism, to say the least. Two French Canadian historians differ from Garneau, and both specifically take him to task. Father Arthur Maheux, a strong champion of *la bonne entente*, views the Conquest not as a Calvary but, implicitly at least, as a resurrection. Marcel Trudel also criticizes Garneau for his unsound judgment, i.e., in calling the military regime a tyranny. Quite the contrary, it was "highly laudable."

General James Murray, the governor of the City of Quebec until 1764, and then the Governor-General of the Colony of

Quebec, is an almost venerable figure in Canadian history. Historians in Canada, of both languages, concur in their views of this irascible, but almost saintly, *good governor.* Murray is the foundation upon which were erected the myths of the good governors. Mahon, his most sympathetic biographer, suggests in addition a little-emphasized aspect of Murray's government and policies, and one which should be further investigated and questioned— how deep were Murray's fingers in the commercial pie that was conquered New France? But let us for now see the facts as presented by Mahon. In Parts III and IV Murray's policies will be further considered.

A. L. Burt, *The Old Province of Quebec*, (Minneapolis, University of Minnesota Press, 1933), pp. 13–56. Reprinted by permission of the author.

The Happy Days of the

Military Regime

The military heel has ground out groans from conquered people in many lands. But the rule of the soldier, though proverbially heavy, was particularly light in Canada during the first few years of British rule. These years are known as the military régime or the *règne militaire*. Until permanently ceded by treaty, Canada was only a temporary possession of uncertain future and, in accordance with the customs of war, was occupied and administered by the victorious army. But the Peace of Paris, which was signed on February 10, 1763, did not terminate this régime at once. It had to be continued until a regular civil government was established, which was not until August 10, 1764. This date was fixed inferentially by one of the terms of the treaty, which gave all Canadians the right to retain their French allegiance by withdrawing from the colony before that time. For eighteen months after the treaty, therefore, the population of Canada could not be regarded as wholly and finally British. Thus the military régime lasted for nearly five years in the district of Quebec and for nearly four years in the rest of the country.

During this period the colony had three governments, each quite independent of the others. The first, that of Quebec, arose immediately after the capital of Canada was captured on September 18, 1759, almost a year before the governments of Montreal and of Three Rivers were established. In his secret instructions Wolfe had been directed to appoint a governor for the place when it fell. This duty now devolved upon General Monckton, who had sufficiently recovered from his wound to resume the command from Townshend. As the latter did not wish to remain, the offer of the governorship was naturally made to the next senior officer, Brigadier General James Murray, who accepted the honor. His appointment was arranged in a "council of war" on September 21, but was not actually made until October 23. At the same time, Monckton appointed Lieutenant Colonel Ralph Burton to be lieutenant governor, and Murray selected Captain Hector Theophilus Cramahé as his secretary. Burton, the son of a Yorkshire attorney, was to leave no impression as lieutenant governor of Quebec, and even though he became military governor of Three Rivers and later of Montreal, and then succeeded to the command of the troops in the colony on the establishment of civil government in 1764, he remains little more than a shadow. Cramahé, on the other hand, became a very much better known figure in the life of the country with whose government he was intimately associated for nearly twenty years as secretary, councillor, acting receiver general, judge, and lieutenant governor. In him Murray made an excellent choice, for he was a businesslike officer, and his French blood, much stronger than the faith he inherited from his Huguenot ancestors, bound him in deep sympathy to the Canadians.

James Murray, as military governor of Quebec and later as the first British governor of Canada, was to leave a much greater mark on the history of the country. He was born in January, 1721, the fifth son of the fourth Lord Elibank of the Scottish peerage. His formal schooling, which lasted until he was fifteen years old, was probably very thorough, for it was all in Scotland, and the letters he wrote in later life bear the stamp of a fine education. There is a family tradition that he was originally destined for the bar, and this may very well be true, for two of his elder brothers entered the army and the other two went into the navy and the church. He left school, however, the year after his father's death, to commence his military career as a cadet in a Scottish unit in the Dutch service, to which he was drawn by family connection. At the age of nineteen he received his first commission in the British army. The time was most auspicious, for Britain was beginning that series of wars that filled the middle years of the eighteenth century and were marked with British victories all over the world. After serving in the West Indies and on the continent of Europe, Murray came to America in 1757 with the rank of lieutenant-colonel and shared in the capture of Louisburg in the following year. He was one of the three brigadiers under General Wolfe, who had a high regard for him. He commanded the left wing of the army in the battle on the Plains of Abraham.

There was not a drop of cold blood in the veins of James Murray. His forceful personality fired men with either love or hate, and he returned their sentiments with equal warmth. Even in this distant day, those who bury themselves in the correspondence of that time feel the spell of his character and have to guard against the temptation to be for him or against him. He had all the pride of a soldier and of a Highlander, and this pride frequently touched off his explosive temper. Some might say that he was ill tempered, but this would hardly be fair, because noble feelings quite as often roused his ire. His sense of justice was as delicate as his pride, and the welfare of those who were placed under his charge was much dearer to him than his own interests. Indeed, the strongest passion which this forthright man was to manifest during his seven years in Canada was pity for the whole Canadian race. This pity was deep-rooted, for he knew more than their tongue: he knew their hearts, and they quickly learned to love him. . . .

. . . Only two months after the capture of Quebec, in a letter to Amherst, Murray struck the keynote of his Canadian career. "Everybody will inform you how powerful and how flourishing this colony was, and how formidable it might be under any other government than that of Monsr. Vaudreuil. *En bonne politique,* it should be perhaps destroyed, but there may be reasons why it should remain, as it is a guarantee for the good behaviour of its neighbouring colonies. It is not with me to judge, I know, it is in your power now to decide the fate of Canada. Until I have the honour to receive your orders, I shall follow the natural disposition of my heart, which dictates clemency. This conduct can do no hurt, because the effects of it may be undone in one week. It may have a permanent advantage. The Canadians have been taught to look upon [us] as barbarians whose only view was their destruction;

hence the obstinate resistance they have made, and the eagerness they shewed to take up arms against us. They begin now to be astonished with our conduct, will soon be convinced that there was no deceit in it, and hardly will hereafter be easily persuaded to take up arms against a nation they admire, and who will have it always in their [power] to burn or destroy. Sufficient examples they have [had] this summer of the horrors of war. They were n[ever] treated tenderly before we had the good fortune to [take] Quebec. They will remember that no doubt and it [may] be supposed they will not forget any instances of [humanity] and generosity that may be shewn them since [they] have been entirely in our power."

Murray was giving voice to more than his own thoughts. He was expressing the feelings of the army under him. Although some soldiers were tempted to continue the war on their own account by plundering the natives, they were exceptions, and at least one of them was hanged as an example to the others. With the fall of Quebec, the barrier of hostility between French and British crumbled. At once the inhabitants of Beauport received the happy soldiers with open arms and made them happier still with wine and such other refreshments as they possessed, and the people generally began to flock in to surrender their arms and make their submission. Just one week after the capitulation, Captain Knox recorded in his journal: "it is with the utmost satisfaction that I have daily ocular experience of the most distinguished humanity and generosity in our worthy soldiers; they not only share their provisions with the distressed Canadians, but even their small allowance of rum: today I saw above twenty of our men assisting those poor people in cutting and binding their

sheaves of corn; they being within the district of the post where I was on duty, I went towards them, and, asking the soldiers what they were to get for their labour, they replied, 'They sought not any thing; what they did was out of good will to the poor creatures, who had little enough for themselves.' One of them added, 'It would be rank murder to take any thing from the poor devils, for they have lost enough already.' While I stood reflecting on the matchless goodness of our honest Britons, with the oddity of the foregoing speech, I saw a peasant take from his pocket a sealskin pouch, which they all refused: one of them instantly produced a rusty iron box that was also filled with tobacco, and tendered it to the Canadian, saying, 'When it is out, I know where to get more; perhaps that is not your case, poor man!' " Nor was the new-found harmony between conqueror and conquered confined to men in the harvest field, as may be inferred from the general orders that were issued shortly to stop soldiers from marrying the inhabitants.

Although a few hearts may have been blighted by this command, countless other hearts were delighted by another command in these same general orders. It enjoined all officers, on meeting religious processions in the streets, "to pay them the compliment of the hat, because it is a civility due to the people who have chosen to live under the protection of our laws"; or, if their Protestant consciences were too sturdy, they were to retire on the approach of any procession. Though the few Jesuit fathers were turned out of their college that it might be used as a storehouse and barrack, the hundred nuns of the General Hospital, the Hôtel Dieu, and the Ursuline Convent were very differently treated, for they were true sisters of mercy to the British garrison. Perhaps prudery as well as pity inspired Ursuline fingers to knit stockings for bare-legged Scots, but no such mixed motives led the inmates of the three houses to care for the sick, whose numbers grew daily until they were well over two thousand. By their tender nursing these sisters did more than save hundreds of British lives. They did much to heal the spiritual wounds that war inflicts, and perhaps contributed more than any other influence to the friendly relations that drew conqueror and conquered together.

In pity for their poverty as well as in gratitude for their Christian services, Monckton gave the nuns of the General Hospital four hundred pounds before he departed, and throughout the winter Murray issued provisions to the three communities and saw that they were supplied with fuel. One incident illustrating their spirit and the governor's attitude is worth special mention. While sitting at a table in the Ursuline Convent, Murray signed the death warrant of a soldier who had broken through the guard protecting the General Hospital and tried to enter the convent. He did not die, however, for the nuns interceded in his behalf and the general pardoned the culprit. Murray's memory, which all the communities of Quebec still cherish, is a touching reminder of the countless civilities that passed at this time. . . .

Amherst had also to provide the colony with a government, for the conquest was followed immediately by an administrative decapitation. All the old salaried officials retired to France with the defeated army. Their withdrawal was natural, since they were not natives of Canada and they hoped for new preferments at home . . .

Another feature of the French régime Amherst did more than continue; he developed it to be the pivot of the government in each locality. This was the captain of militia, who was transformed into a British functionary by the receipt of a new commission, his old one having become invalid with the cession of the country. At once he was ordered to assemble the male inhabitants to disarm them and to administer the oath of allegiance. He himself, however, was allowed to retain a firelock to assist in preserving good order and discipline in his village, for he was to be its policeman. He also became its magistrate. This new function he acquired as a consequence of Amherst's desire to have all disputes between the inhabitants settled, as much as possible, among themselves and by their own laws. Of course there were bound to be some cases too difficult to be determined by this general factotum of the government in each parish; and these, according to Amherst's orders, were to be brought before the British officer commanding in the locality, who in turn was to submit them when necessary to the military governor. The jurisdiction of the captain of militia also stopped short of serious crimes, such as theft and murder, for which, as might be expected, the commander-in-chief prescribed military law.

Amherst's concern for the Canadians appears in the following injunction, which he issued to Murray, Gage, and Burton. "As the inhabitants of this country are now as much His Majesty's subjects as any of us, and so long as they remain deserving of it, are entitled to the same protection, I would have you particularly give it in charge to the troops under your command to live in good harmony and brotherhood with them and to avoid all differences whatsoever." The same feeling is more fully revealed by a documents one leading motive runs, the enlightenment of the people. This document bears the date September 22, and is known as a "placard," because it was posted up all over the country at the doors of the churches. While proclaiming the disarmament of the population, it invited all who desired arms for hunting to apply to their respective military governors, or their deputies, for permits to enjoy this privilege. It announced the continuance of their old captains of militia and the new authority with which these officials were invested. . . .

In theory the military governors may have been autocrats whose will was law, subject of course to the revision of the commander-in-chief. In fact the relation between their will and the law was the very reverse. Their will was expressed in proclamations, ordinances, orders, decrees, and commissions. But these names, except the last, were used rather indiscriminately, for the military governors' training and position made them careless of the civilian's distinction between the judicial, the administrative, and the legislative functions of government. Many of these public documents issued by Murray have not been found, but the loss is probably of no great moment. The corresponding documents for Montreal and for Three Rivers have been preserved, and to these two collections, between which there is very little difference, the surviving Quebec fragments bear a close resemblance. In the absence of any contrary evidence, therefore, one may presume that Murray exercised his authority in much the same manner as did the other military governors. Through all these document which he prepared for the preservation of Canadian society as it was found on the morrow of the conquest.

Not only the laws but also the customs that held this society together were maintained with as little change as possible. . . .

Under the French régime the intervention of the intendant had been necessary to keep the feudal system working properly. Now that he was gone, who was there to take over this function unless it was the military governor? This question faced Gage almost at once, and he did not hesitate to assume the intendant's power. For some years the growing inflation of the currency had been lifting the burden of feudal dues. When real money appeared on the morrow of the conquest, seigniors naturally objected to tenants getting rid of their pecuniary obligations and their worthless paper at the same time. An appeal to the military governor of Montreal roused Gage's sense of justice. On January 22, 1761, he published a general order requiring all seigniorial *rentes*, and also *lods et ventes*, to be paid in metallic currency, except where contracts stipulated otherwise. All inhabitants were to "repair on the day to the place and at the hour, which will be notified to them by the captains of the respective seigneuries, with their contracts and last receipts, for the purpose of paying the arrears of rent, which they may owe, on pain of proceedings against the defaulters, as is customary." The presumption is that his word was obeyed, for it was not repeated, as were some other decrees that were difficult to enforce.

As might be expected, the habitants of the Montreal district were not the only ones who sought to ease their feudal burden by using the old paper. In the previous November the Quebec court, on receiving a petition transmitted by Murray, had already decreed that *cens et rentes* be paid in hard cash. Similar action may have been taken in Three Rivers, though there is no record of it. In the spring of 1762, again on seigniorial appeals, Gage applied the fifty-year-old *Arrêt* of Marly, under which habitants lost the holdings they failed to occupy and to improve within a year and a day of their concession. He gave the delinquents anywhere from six months' to a year's warning. Sometimes this was effective. Sometimes it was not, and then, on the local militia captain's certifying that the proper notice had been read and posted at the parish church with no result, the governor issued a final decree.

It is not known whether the new rulers of Three Rivers and of Quebec also put this old law into operation. Possibly the abandonment of conceded holdings was confined to the upper district, where the lure of the fur trade had an unsettling influence. In both Montreal and Three Rivers the governors were besought to carve out new seigniories from the uncultivated lands, and to avoid trenching on any ancient grants they ordered all who had French titles to uncleared fiefs to present these titles on pain of forfeiture. In Quebec, Murray also faced the demand for new seigniories, and throughout the colony homage was performed as before the conquest. Nor were the feudal rights of the crown forgotten. To discover all the mutation fines that might fall due —the *quint* on fiefs and the *lods et ventes* on land held of the king *en roture*—the notaries of Montreal and of Three Rivers, and possibly also those of Quebec, were ordered to submit copies of all sales and transfers for which they supplied the necessary instruments.

These notaries constituted another essential feature of Canadian society. They drew up all conveyances of land and other property, bonds for the payment of money, deeds of partnership, marriage contracts, and generally all written agreements intended to be legally binding. Their houses were offices of record where all the original documents were deposited. Though only attested copies were given to the interested parties, such copies had as great validity in Canadian courts as the originals would have had in English courts. These men were not private individuals but public functionaries commissioned, though not paid, by the government, and therefore they were officially known as royal notaries. They were scattered all over the country in almost every parish, and as a body they formed the corner stone of private property throughout the colony. . . .

In approaching the currency question, Burton followed blindly in Murray's footsteps. Within a few days of his appointment to the government of Three Rivers he forbade paying or receiving in payment the old paper, which he dubbed "imaginary money." This was the last official effort to destroy all faith in the preconquest circulating medium. No denunciation was ever issued in Montreal, where Amherst advised caution, and both in Quebec and in Three Rivers the governors relented from their stern attitude. The surrender of the country transformed what had been good propaganda into bad politics. Now the military governors naturally sought to foster the welfare and to cultivate the good will of the people under their care. Had they continued to insist that this money possessed no value, they would have been working to wipe out the capital of many and the savings of all. Moreover, they would have been putting themselves in a false position, for this money still had some value, small though it might be, based on the promise of deferred payment. But they could not establish any equivalence between this doubtful paper and the other currency, the value of which rested on the bullion it contained. Such official action would have disturbed the economic life of the colony, and it might have incurred the risk of involving the British government in the obligations of the French government. Therefore, with the exception noted below, they held aloof from the whole business, leaving the people free to accept this paper for what they might think it was worth. The courts, however, could not shut their eyes to its daily use. Sitting in judgment upon cases of debt incurred in terms of the old currency, they had to insist upon payment in paper or its market value in coin. After some fluctuations, the discount settled at about eighty-five per cent, at which rate not only Canadians but also English-speaking merchants who had followed in the wake of the army were glad to receive the paper. From them it passed into the hands of London merchants, who naturally pressed their government to insist upon the French government redeeming its obligations.

This discussion of the matter during the peace negotiations in 1762 raised hopes of justice in Canada and of profit in London. Seeing the conflict between these two hopes, the military governors threw their weight in favor of the former by trying to dissuade the Canadians from parting with their paper at a sacrifice. In this year one of the London schemers, an army contractor named Arnold Nesbit, was so brazen that he wrote to Murray offering to share the profit on thirty thousand pounds' worth of Canadian paper which he contemplated purchasing because he had private information from Paris that some liquidation was contemplated. The insulted governor at once summoned the leading Canadians, and to

them he read the letter, adding many an eloquent comment of his own. The immediate result of this disclosure was that paper jumped two hundred per cent in the local market, and the permanent effect was that Murray incurred the undying hatred of many British traders. In the following year, when the French plenipotentiary signed, along with the treaty, a declaration promising payment, the military governors published it throughout Canada and called upon all holders of paper to register it according to the procedure stipulated by the French government. The registration was performed gratis.

In regulating the metallic currency, the governors of Three Rivers and of Montreal did not follow Murray's example. In place of the Halifax standard of five shillings to the dollar, which he had adopted and now maintained, they accepted the New York system of eight shillings to the dollar, which Amherst introduced by implication in his famous placard. That York currency, as it was commonly called, should prevail in these two governments was natural, because their business connection was largely with New York over the Lake Champlain route. It also had the advantage of coinciding with the division of the Spanish dollar into eight *reals*, or "bits." The convenience of this reckoning in the two upper governments was probably greater than it would have been in Quebec, where there seems to have been a greater variety of coins. . . .

To meet his greater needs, Murray found greater resources. Though he unearthed an old tax on all houses in the city for the maintenance of the barracks, he could not use it. So many houses and so many people had been ruined by two sieges in one year that he felt the necessity of giving rather than of taking. On the advice of his military court or council, he taxed the country people to relieve the distress of the townsfolk, who had lost everything they had possessed and yet were obliged to lodge the British garrison. The tax was one dollar for each horse and was collected from the parishes "least burdened with troops or with supplying carriages for their use." It was levied but once and brought six hundred pounds, which was distributed among the more necessitous proprietors of the buildings Murray had appropriated for public use. This transaction is interesting because it reflects a considerable prosperity in the rural district of Quebec. The amount raised represents twenty-four hundred horses, and horses were much of a luxury, the land being tilled by horned cattle. The incident is also worth noting because of the use to which it was afterwards put. In later days Murray's bitter enemies charged him with levying illegal taxes, and cited this as an example. There was certainly no precedent for the imposition, but his military council advised it, and, considering the circumstances, none but a legal pedant could condemn it.

Two other sources peculiar to Quebec which the head of that government uncovered provided a steady income based upon the authority of the past. One of these was the King's Posts. Ainslie's management brought sufficient promise of profit to inspire Murray to write home to the treasury urging the lease of this trade. On receiving a favorable reply he turned the posts over, in September, 1762, to Thomas Dunn and John Gray for one year certain and for a further period of fourteen years unless contrary orders arrived from Great Britain, in return for four hundred pounds a year. Murray's enemies later said that this was a nice gift to his friends. But four hundred pounds a year was much more than the French government had ever got for these posts. Also it was essential that they be placed in trustworthy hands, as they were. Both the lessees were very respectable merchants, and one of them, Dunn, was to rise high in the service of the Canadian government.

The other source of revenue that Murray found was the customs duties. As these were the old king's rights, they became the new king's rights, and therefore the governor was entitled to demand them. He saw, however, that the old tariff would work many injuries, and consequently he whittled it down to one item. On November 22, 1760, he published an order enforcing a duty of sixpence a gallon on all spirituous liquors. Early in the following summer, mercantile arguments in favor of British traders and British shipping moved him to exempt spirits manufactured in Britain, which meant that rum from the old colonies was about the only drink to be taxed. To Murray's enemies this duty was a most flagrant violation of the law, but the only flaw the lawyers later found was that sixpence a gallon was slightly higher than the old rate on rum, though less than what had been charged on other alcoholic goods. On Murray's behalf it should also be observed that he had the tacit approval of the treasury, to which he reported the steps he was taking and to which he accounted annually for his collections and disbursements.

On looking back over all the enactments of the military régime, one is struck by the fact that the governors did more than follow the forms of the old régime. They caught its best spirit. They speak not as conquerors to a subject race, but as fathers to their children; their words are less stern commands than paternal admonitions. . . .

The records of this military régime make it stand out unique in the annals of occupied territories. From the very beginning of the period the inhabitants were astonished at the lenity of their new masters and were delighted that the war had stopped with the fighting. *"Ces nobles vainqueurs ne parvient-ils pas de lors oublier qu'ils avoient été nos ennemis, pour ne s'occuper que de nos besoins et des moyens efficaces d'y subvenir!"* These words to all the faithful under his charge, uttered by the vicar general of Quebec, Briand, are but one of the many expressions of gratitude which the Canadians poured out in glowing terms.

The reasons for this wonderful harmony between conquered and conqueror are not far to seek. One of the most important causes was the very completeness of the British victory. It banished from the minds of the British the fear which might have been the father of cruelty. It was also a powerful incentive to submission on the part of the Canadians. Their submission was made more whole-hearted by the thought that France had deserted them and by the realization of the blessings which the British bestowed. These blessings were liberty, prosperity, and peace, and the greatest of these was peace. For this they had been longing with all their hearts. Though many had been stricken by the scourge of war, prosperity now returned, and it was greater than any they had ever known. And the liberty they now breathed inspired new life in them. No more cramping monopolies! No more oppressive extortions by government servants! They even disputed the tithes with their clergy.

Highly fortunate it was that the final treaty did not come swift on the heels of the capitulation, for then civilians would have tried their hands at the task of governing Canada, and they would probably have made a sorry mess of it. Civilian minds steeped in the tradition of English law would have disturbed the even tenor of Canadian ways by attempting to change the laws and customs of the country, for this is what they did at the close of the military régime. Heaven was kind to Britain and to Canada in keeping the army there. The army healed the wounds it had inflicted, and this is the best healing. Its leaders were blinded by no legal prejudices and so did not interfere with the complex organism of Canadian society. They gave the Canadians the finest quality of liberty—the liberty to be themselves. They did it by rule of thumb; they did it out of the pity that was in their hearts; they did it consciously and unconsciously on the great principle enunciated by Egremont. In the interest of the British Empire and of Canada the Canadians were to be won, and they were won.

Of all the glorious victories that British armies have to their credit, none is more glorious, none is more honorable, than the moral conquest that crowned the military conquest of Canada. The years of this military régime are of supreme importance in the history of Canada, for they planted in Canadian hearts that trust in British justice which has preserved the country with its dual nationality from splitting asunder.

These years are also a watershed in the history of the British Empire, for the French in Canada were the first considerable body of an alien race to taste that liberty which is larger than English liberty and is the secret of the modern British commonwealth of nations.

"Ordinances, Proclamations . . . Issued by the Military Governors of Quebec, Montreal and Trois-Rivières from the Capitulation of Quebec Until the Establishment of Civil Government . . . , *Report of the Public Archives of Canada,* 1918, (Ottawa, 1918), pp. 2–126.

Proclamations by the

Military Governors

Open your eyes, Canadians, to your own interests, all communication with the Ocean being blocked, what can you expect of an army, weak, beaten and dispirited; without hope or resource, with a great army of disciplined troops in the heart of the country, another at its gates, nearly all the posts in the upper country captured or abandoned.

We exhort you eagerly to have recourse to a people, free, honest and generous, ready to stretch out its arms to you, to set you free from a harsh despotism, and to enable you to enjoy with them the comforts of a government, just, mild and equitable. For if you do not profit by this advice, you must expect the most rigorous treatment, which is permissible by the laws of war.

The manifestos of Generals Wolfe and Monckton have breathed the kindliest and most humane sentiments; also, their menaces were just. These menaces have not so far been carried into effect, since it was known that every effort was made to induce Canadians to believe the English to be a race without honour or humanity. At this period, they should feel how much they have been imposed upon. Our conduct towards those of their compatriots, who have surrendered to us, establishes this fact. Therefore, since there is no longer an excuse for Canadians, if they should resolve to have recourse to arms, they must expect all the severity which it is in the power of a victorious but justly irritated army to exercise. The blame will fall on themselves. Such a line of conduct will be dictated by human nature, and it will be fully justified by the laws of nations.

Done at Quebec, November 15, 1759.

And sealed with the seal of our arms.

(A copy)

H. T. CRAMAHÉ,
Secretary.

By His Excellency James Murray.

As we desire to establish order and police in the country, we have thought fit to publish the following orders, to serve as regulations for the inhabitants, and enjoin them to conform strictly thereto, under penalty of being punished as disobedient.

(1) As soon as night sets in, the inhabitants of the town, who are on the streets, will carry a light in their hands, after tattoo sounds they will not leave their houses, and at nine o'clock the lights in all houses will be extinguished.

(2) If fire breaks out in a house, the occupant will notify the Commander of the District without delay, and will, at the same time, take all necessary measures to extinguish it.

(3) When strangers come to the town, the inhabitants whose houses they enter will take care to notify our secretary immediately, in order that they may be examined.

(4) Colonel Young, who dwells near Government House is appointed Judge of the cases and disputes, which may arise among the inhabitants, and will sit for this purpose at his house on Tuesday and Friday mornings from nine o'clock until noon.

(5) All inhabitants are at liberty to take from the town all sorts of goods, except munitions of war, food, leather of any kind, soap and candles, for which they will have to obtain passports from our secretary. All kinds of provisions may be brought freely into the town, and those who bring them will be particularly encouraged.

(6) Communication within the town is free; and the sentries at the outer gates or barriers are the only ones, who have orders to stop people.

(7) If any soldier offers the least injury or insult to an inhabitant, the latter will take his complaint without loss of time to the first guardhouse, the officers in charge of which will have orders to hold the soldier, and put him under arrest, until the complaint can be dealt with.

(8) All complaints which the inhabitants may have to lay before us, or favours, which they may have occasion to request, should be put in writing in the form of a plea, and delivered to our secretary during his office hours, to be submitted by him to us, in order that, twice a week, we may examine and reply to them.

In those first moments of confusion, one could not put all the order into affairs, which was desirable, and we are but too fully persuaded that wrong was being done to many poor inhabitants. But at this time when we are more settled, we are determined to maintain a strict and rigid discipline, and to punish with the utmost severity all who may be convicted of having done the slightest injury. In testimony whereof, we have signed these presents and caused the seal of our arms to be affixed thereto—at Quebec this 15th of November 1759.

(a copy)

H. T. CRAMAHÉ,
Secretary.

By His Excellency James Murray, &c.

As an interchange of correspondence by letter is taking place between Montreal, the Western Posts and this part of Canada very prejudicial to the service of His Britannic Majesty, we deem it proper to declare by these presents that we forbid, under penalty of death, any person of whatever quality or condition he may be to deliver any letters to any persons whatever, before they have been delivered to us to be examined, and we declare that those who receive such letters before they have been delivered to us, as above ordered, will undergo the same punishment. We likewise order under the same penalties all persons residing in the part of Canada under subjection to His Britannic Majesty to act in the same manner regarding the letters which they may have occasion to send beyond the advance posts of our army.

Done at Quebec January 12, 1760.

And sealed with the seal of our arms.

(a copy)

H. T. CRAMAHÉ,
Secretary.

By His Excellency James Murray,
Esquire.

As we have knowledge of many articles of merchandise, which have been secretly carried from this town on several occasions, notwithstanding that the conveyance out, without passport, has been expressly prohibited by the ordinance issued on the 15th November last, in order to put an end to this abuse, we deem it proper to declare and we do declare that after the date of the present, all persons, of whatever rank or condition they may be, are forbidden to cause anything to be taken from this town, without a passport signed by our secretary, under penalty of death to those who are convicted of having contravened the regulation.

Done at Quebec—January 12, 1760.

And sealed with the seal of our arms.

(A copy)

H. T. CRAMAHÉ,
Secretary.

By His Excellency James Murray, &c.

Being justly irritated at the treachery of those of the inhabitants of Point Levy, who in disregard of the oath which they have taken and of the protection with which they have been favored by us, have for two consecutive nights concealed a large detachment of the enemy without informing us of them.

For this reason we are determined to chastise them with severity.

This chastisement is just and necessary to prevent the embarrassments, which may result if this crime remained unpunished, and to stop others from falling in a similar case.

Those should be held responsible, who, by their efforts, as feeble as they were powerless, instead of saving Canada, are bringing it to ruin.

We did not wish to listen to the first notices we received of the want of faith of these unfortunate people, it was not until their second offence that we resolved to punish them for it.

We promise again all the inhabitants of Canada, those under our rule, as well as those of the upper parishes, to protect with all our force, those who as good citizens remain quietly at their homes. As we declare solemnly that we shall take a striking vengeance upon those who dare to take up arms.

Done at Quebec February 26, 1760.

And sealed with the seal of our arms.

(A copy)

H. T. CRAMAHÉ,
Secretary.

By His Excellency James Murray.

We are at last furnished with authority by His Majesty. In consequence we seize with joy the earliest moment to declare to Canadians his benevolent desires respecting them.

A gracious and kindly prince, the father and protector of all his subjects, speaks to them through me.

Adhering to his promises religiously, he will violate none of them.

Those who submitting to the circumstances, have taken the oath of fidelity to him, and who, faithful to their oath, have yielded with a good grace to the orders of those to whom he has delegated his power, can feel assured of his protection.

They will be made secure in their property, their religious and civil status, and the religious communities will enjoy all their privileges. . . .

By His Excellency James Murray, etc.

We have given the inhabitants the time necessary to come to themselves and to reflect seriously on the folly of their conduct.

They have neglected our salutary advice, and, trusting to deceitful appearances, have drawn upon themselves, fresh misfortunes.

If we listened only to our just resentment, for a course so unexampled they would deserve the severest chastisement, but guided by more humane sentiments, we wish to try to withdraw them from the abyss into which they have plunged. We are not unaware of the tricks and artifices, which have been employed to ensnare them and which in some measure, furnish their excuse.

In a word, the most generous people in the world stretch out their arms to them a second time, and offer them powerful and unfailing assistance.

Their past faults will be overlooked on condition that hereafter they will, by irreproachable conduct, make themselves worthy of so distinguished a clemency.

The King, my master, who is resolved to gain possession of Canada has no desire to reign over a depopulated province.

He wishes to preserve for the inhabitants, the religion they cherish and the priests, who exercise it, to maintain the communities and private individuals in all their property, laws and customs, provided that, satisfied with sentiments so generous, they submit willingly and promptly to his orders.

France is impotent, and is unable to furnish assistance to them.

The fleet, annihilated by the defeats of Conflans and La Clue, dare not come out.

Unpaid Bills of exchange, and the complete discredit of a contemptible and useless paper money offer to this colony nothing but an endless chain of misfortunes.

It has no resources except in our people, who, rich and flourishing, abound in everything.

But they must deserve our benefits; the inhabitants cannot return to the town nor partake with us the blessings, which come from our continent, until all have made submission.

Canadians! Withdraw from the army, put down your arms, remain in your homes, and give no assistance to our enemies; on these conditions your tranquillity will not be interrupted; you will carry on your labours in safety, the soldiery will be restrained, the fields will not be destroyed; you still have time to avoid famine and the plague, scourges of Heaven, more ravenous than those of war, and which at present, threaten Canada with total and irreparable ruin.

Done at Quebec May 22, 1760.

And sealed with the seal of our arms.

(A copy)

H. T. CRAMAHÉ,
Secretary.

Description of two servants, who have deserted.

[November 29.]

Description of two servants who deserted from the house of Major Christie, on the night between the 24th and 25th instant, having carried off with them some household articles.

One Thomas Lloyd, English by birth, a young man of 17 years of age, 5 feet 4 inches in height, rather well built, slender legs, hair and eyebrows light, face long and pale, and he speaks rather poor

French. He wore, when he escaped, a livery of blue cloth lined with red serge with redplush facings, and white flat buttons, a scarlet vest, and trousers of dressed skin with a black velvet cap.

And one John Mora, Canadian of Quebec, of about 18 years of age, of 5 feet 7 inches in height, a white, clear skinned face, a high, turned-up nose, hair and eyebrows light; he wore, when he escaped, a brown cloak, a blue vest lined with white, green trousers, a hat with high rim, and a frock coat of grey cloth.

It is enjoined &c. Ten dollars' reward for those, who may arrest the said deserters, or five dollars for one of the two.

Description of two servants, who deserted from the residence of Major Christie at Montreal.
[May 23, 1762]
Jonhs Raab, German, slender, about five feet seven inches in height, bloodshot eyes, very dark, long black hair ordinarily in tresses, wears a green suit, and a piece of green ribbon as a cockade in his hat, which has a silver-bound edge.

David King, a German about five feet five inches, well built, red hair, heavily freckled, wears plain red clothes, and breeches of buckskin; both speak French but bad English.

N.B. They took off with them a blue frock coat with white buttons.

At Trois-Rivières this 23rd May, 1762.

Six dollars' reward for those who arrest and deliver them to Major Christie at Montreal.

By order of Colonel Haldimand.

L. MÉTRAL,

Town Major.

F.-X. Garneau, *Histoire du Canada de-puis sa découverte jusqu'à nos jours,* Vol. 3, (Québec, N. Aubin, 1845-48), pp. 295-301, 303-310, 312-313 (Translated C.N.)

The Military Regime:

A Tyranny

The Canadians who had not left the army after the siege of Quebec abandoned it after the capitulation of Montreal, and a most profound peace soon reigned in all of the country. One would not have known that a bloody war had just ended, if so many parts of Canada had not borne the scars of ravages and ruin, especially in the Government of Quebec. . . . The inhabitants, ruined but proud of having fulfilled their duty towards their country to the last moment, thought only of returning to their lands to repair their losses and isolating themselves as much as possible from the new government. They appeared to want . . . to occupy themselves exclusively with agriculture.

The conquerors, having achieved their precious conquest, occupied themselves with the means of conserving it. . . . Canada was treated as a barbarous nation without an established government and without laws. It was divided into three departments corresponding to the three divisions of the French regime, and

received a purely military administration. . . . Murray was placed at the head of that of Quebec, . . . Gage, . . . Montreal . . . [and] Three Rivers fell to . . . Burton . . .

They immediately began the task of reorganization, but each proceeded differently. General Murray established a council or military tribunal composed of seven army officers, which sat twice a week and rendered decisions upon the most important civil and criminal affairs; as for the others, he reserved the right of adjudicating them himself without appeal. For this purpose he held open court in his residence once a week, his secretary fulfilling the function of recorder. Control over regulations in the countryside was surrendered to the local commandants. General Gage appears to have wished to soften this arbitrary system a little: he authorized the captains of the parish to settle the differences that might arise between the citizens, with the reservation of a right of appeal to the military commander of the area . . . The Canadians, by the means of their militia officers, thus found themselves taking part in the administration of justice in the Government of Montreal. But in that of Quebec, they participated only through two men of law taken from their own group. . . .

This was the military regime established in Canada immediately after the end of hostilities, in direct violation of the terms of the capitulation, which guaranteed to the Canadians the rights of English subjects, rights by which the laws could not be changed, nor could persons be judged by other than their natural judges without their consent. Thus, where they thought to live under a legal government in the shadow of peace, they saw their tribunals abolished, their judges kept at bay, their laws unknown or forgotten and all their old social regime overturned and replaced by the most abject tyranny, that of a state of siege and of martial courts. There is nothing that contributed more to isolate the government from the population than this conduct repudiated so long ago by public rights and the usages of nations. Knowing neither the language, nor the customs, nor the character of the conquering people, the Canadians fled the judges . . . appointed among them, and who did not even have learning to recommend them . . . By a happy set of circumstances the people and clergy found common interests, and beneath the sway of the sword moral evangelism became the law of this population firmly united by the instinct of self-preservation.

This military organization, which is testimony to the fear that the long and glorious resistance of Canada had inspired, was approved by the new metropolis, on the condition, however, that it would last only till the re-establishment of peace: and then, if the country continued in its possession, a civil government would be established. We remained thus under martial law for four years. This period is known in our annals by the name of *Military Regime*.

However, the Canadians persisted in believing, no doubt because they desired it, that France would not wish to abandon them, and that she would have the colony returned to her at the peace. They waited for the happy news at every moment with a high hope, but they were deceived in this deepest of their wishes. The Treaty of 1763, assuring the possession of Canada to Great Britain, led to a new migration. The merchants, the lawyers, the former administrators, and finally most of the notable families of the country went to France, after having sold or even abandoned possessions which today are still the object of disputes among their descendants. There remained in the cities only a few subordinate employees, a few artisans, hardly one merchant, and the religious community. This emigration did not extend to the countryside where the inhabitants were tied to the land.

. . . Those who remained in Canada hoped, in the light of the promise of their new metropolis, to obtain eventually a regular government. In spite of the fact that under the military regime French law and the French language were adopted in legal matters, the system did not offer any lasting guarantees. As well, a new radical change took place in 1764; but, far from relieving the burden that rested upon the unhappy country, it made it even more intolerable. Every day the Canadians learned more and more fully all the ill effects of subjugation to the foreigner, and that the sacrifices they had made were nothing in comparison with the sufferings and the moral humiliations being prepared for them and for their posterity. First, England wanted to repudiate all that was French and even take away from the original inhabitants the natural advantages offered them by their country in order to establish its own children. . . .

At the same time, Murray was named Governor-General . . . The new governor, in obedience to his instructions, soon formed a council invested, jointly with him, with executive, legislative and judicial powers. He lacked only the right to impose taxes. This body, composed of eight members, contained only a single inhabitant of the country, an obscure man without influence, chosen only to make up the required number. A jealous and hateful narrowness had dictated these instructions from England, and it is in this sombre document that was born the pro-

found racial antipathy in Canada, noted
in our day by Lord Durham, and that
served him for a pretext to preach a new
persecution against the French Canadians.

. . . General Murray, while severe,
was an honourable man and had a sensitive and generous heart. He liked these
Canadians, so docile to authority like old
soldiers, . . . these brave inhabitants so
simple in their *mores*. . . .

Faced by the aggressive and military
people he was called to govern, conditions
were very difficult for this administrator
who had an open rather than a subtle
character. He was obliged to act surrounded by officials whose conduct made
him blush every day. A flood of adventurers, intriguers, army valets, had descended on Canada in the *suite* of the
English troops and after the capitulation
of Montreal. . . . Merchants of dubious
reputation and tavern-keepers composed
the largest part of this class. Men of pro-
bity and honour formed only a small part.
It was with these tools that he was to
denationalize the country, to establish

new laws and institutions in place of the
old ones which had been discarded, in
order to repeat in Canada what had been
done in Ireland, that is, to drive the
natives from the government and replace
them with strangers. . . . All the public
officials, the judges, and the juries were
English and Protestant. These last even
wanted to have applied the proscriptions
that had been decreed against Catholics
in England. . . .

However, despite all the concessions
to their claims, these greedy strangers
were still not satisfied with the privileges
which they enjoyed; they were furious
that Murray would not grant them an
elective chamber, and made great cla-
mours because he deprived them of constitutional rights they held by birth and
which they said they brought everywhere
with them. It was impossible to comply
with their requests because they wanted
to be the only electors and the only ones
eligible because of the English law that
interdicted Catholic political rights. . . .

Arthur Maheux, *French Canada and Britain: a New Interpretation*, (Toronto, Ryerson Press, 1942), pp. 4-6, 18-21, 25-28. Reprinted by permission of the Ryerson Press, Toronto.

Have Our People Been Unfortunate?

To preserve themselves just as they were, that was the objective which Garneau assigned to the French Canadian people. This meant making tradition, even prejudice, and the imitation of others the masters of our destiny. When romanticism made the shedding of tears the fashion, our people seemed to transform themselves into a languishing, sorrowful, timorous, and impotent René, into a lugubrious chorus with its leader our own Crémazie.

Is this disease incurable? No, certainly not. And because it is not it is up to us to utilize history to inspire our youth with a very positive notion of equality between the two groups in Canada.

François Xavier Garneau attained maturity when French romanticism was at its height. The illustrious author of our national history could scarcely escape the romanticist influence. A study of Garneau's work from that point of view would be very instructive. Let no one see in this assertion, however, any note of blame as it is merely a statement of fact. Garneau surrounded himself with scientific precautions—one of his great merits—and in that he followed the example of the masters whom he had chosen for himself. Another influence, though, that of romanticism, was leaving its mark on nearly everything written in France at that time, . . .

In this way history turned rapidly into lyricism, and among the lyrical species preference was given to elegy. This explains the very marked tendency of some of our historical works to be filled with numerous plaints, to become, indeed, elegiac rosaries wherein our misfortunes are bemoaned over and over. Sturdy, vigorous history gave way to a tearful tale which we are invited to read and meditate upon in the shade of a weeping willow, rather than under a maple, an elm, or an oak. When you have turned the last page you feel bound to say to yourself: How many difficulties Champlain had! How many trials Mgr. de Laval had to endure! How Bigot made us suffer! How much the English have wronged us! We are asked to believe that our people have always been unfortunate, that ill luck has clung to them, that adversity has attended their every effort.

Does this somber portrayal correspond to reality? Have our misfortunes been so great as that? Are the stages of our development all marked by a long succession of funereal monuments? Is every high point in our national career a Calvary? . . .

Let us look back for a moment at the tragic days of 1759, so that we may make a better evaluation of the situation in which the French Canadians found themselves after the death of Montcalm. . . . What did England represent to those people? To the Frenchman of France she was the age-long enemy, though circumstances had at times brought the two rivals somewhat closer together. But to the Frenchman in America, to the Canadian, the Englishman was the constant foe. Between New France and New England animosity was sharpest of all, and Canadians well knew that with victory in their hands English colonials would have scant pity for Frenchmen and "Papists."

There was, perhaps, some hope in the international law of the time, but what security did it offer? And, moreover, did our ancestors know of its existence? Let us take up the first of these two questions. The phrase "International Law" was as yet unknown. One spoke rather of the "law of peoples," and more especially of the "law of war and peace." The whole idea was, in fact, of rather recent growth being only a century and a half old.

A Dutchman, Hugo van Groote, better known as Grotius, was the first to compile all the juridical and historical texts on the relations between nations. . . .

Grotius' celebrated treatise is divided into three parts. In the first part are to be found the definitions of war, just war, and revolt. In the second part, which is longer, those laws whose violation may bring war are studied. And in the third part the author considers the conduct of war. This treatise was deemed authoritative in matters of international law at the time when our forefathers had to change their political allegiance. At this point, then, the second question arises, did our ancestors know about Grotius' work?

The answer must be in the affirmative. . . .

Now what did the code say? This we may discover in Part III where Grotius takes five chapters to discuss the

enemy's rights in a legitimate war, rights founded upon custom and ancient texts. Those seventy-five pages leave but little hope to the vanquished. Briefly, the enemy had the right, according to Grotius, to kill any combatant, all foreigners seized in hostile territory, and all old men, women and children; to pollute drinking water with lime or dead bodies; to reduce all prisoners to slavery, or to kill them even though they may have given themselves up voluntarily; to ravage the countryside, including farms, and raze towns. No exception is made of sacred things; the enemy can destroy churches, pillage their treasures, and even plunder tombs. No restraint is placed upon the seizure of goods and chattels by the conquering armies. Finally, the conqueror possesses the right of absolute sovereignty over the conquered. . . .

It must be pointed out, though, that the capitulation left open two doors to the future. In the first place certain terms were asked "until a final treaty" should be concluded between the two powers. This meant that people still hoped to see France victorious in America, or, more particularly, in Europe. In that event New France would resume its normal prewar existence. But our ancestors also took into account the worst possible eventuality, that of the end of French rule in America. We may see this in Article Six which concerns religion. In that they ask for special protection for the Bishop of Quebec who, they say, "out of zeal for religion, out of charity for the people of his diocese, wishes to remain permanently." Thus the Bishop took his stand. Whatever the outcome of the war he desired to remain with his flock, believing that his presence in Canada would be necessary to uphold the Catholic religion in the event of a shift in political allegiance.

When the eleven articles of the capitulation had been drawn up, citizens and officers alike must have wondered whether the conqueror would grant them all. That was the moment of greatest concern. Finally the die was cast. An emissary set out for the English camp with two copies of the document. That was at noon on September 17. The night passed without a reply. This came only the next day, September 18. Townsend and Saunders had granted all the requests except permission for the garrison to rejoin the French army. Thus our forefathers obtained their desire, an honorable surrender, and, probably, more than they counted upon getting. The Canadians kept their houses, lands, furniture, animals, clothes and tools. They could carry on their religion, and they could not be deported.

Fear of deportation was very strong. Article 5 of the Capitulation reads: "the said inhabitants shall not be transported nor required to leave their homes." Transported is not so harsh a term as deported, but in reality it means the same thing. Scarcely four years had passed since the deportation of the Acadians, an event which the people of Quebec could not forget as they had welcomed some of these Acadians to their city and received them into their homes. What Lawrence had perpetrated in 1755 Townsend, Saunders, and Amherst could also do. Article 5 in itself shows us clearly enough what state of mind New France was in at that moment. It reveals a very clear distinction between the French proper and the Canadians. The former knew quite well what would happen to them. The victor would embark them upon vessels along with the garrison, that is the troops and the sailors, "to be set down at the nearest

port in France." But what would be the fate of the Canadians? Born in America, some recently, but others, indeed the greater number established for three, four, five or more generations, they had no connections in France, not even relatives able to receive and harbor them. Their country, their only country, was America. If the conqueror did not want to let them live in New France where would they go? Some, it is true, would agree to go to France, even though it would be an entirely new country for them, and meant a veritable transplanting. The others, however, would not want to leave for France, but would prefer some corner of America, say an island in the Antilles, Louisiana, or even one of the English colonies.

The Frenchmen in charge of the administration of New France knew all this well enough. They foresaw that the bulk of Canadians would prefer to stay in Canada even though they had to become British subjects. This was the reason for the request that the Canadians be allowed to retain their lands, goods, effects, religion and bishop.

But would the English accord these privileges? Or would they repeat the cruel stroke of 1755? We may well believe that the hours of waiting seemed long, from noon on September 17 till the next morning when the messenger came back with the document signed by the English officers. We can imagine the conversations that went on, the plans that were sketched out about likely places to settle, and the means of getting there. Some would quickly make up their minds to quit the country,—those whose houses had been burned, or destroyed by cannon balls; those who had lost all their money through Bigot's devilish misdoing; those whose only possession was the clothing they wore. For the others who still had their lands, their houses, a few animals and hopes of a harvest, it was harder to think of going away.

When the news spread about that all the terms of the surrender had been granted except the one concerning the French garrison there was unquestionably tremendous relief. The civilians and militiamen who were in the city only for military purposes hastened to their homes in the country. A fair number of Quebec citizens also left the city with the hope of finding in the country the food and shelter that their city could no longer provide for them. Those who chose to remain in Quebec busied themselves with the task of reorganizing their lives, rebuilding their homes, and finding food. People began to lose fear of the conqueror. The majority were doubtless grateful for the enemy's generosity and began to think that it would be possible to get along with these English Protestants.

Shortly after red coats appeared in the city. In accordance with the terms of capitulation [Article 9] English soldiers were placed on guard before churches, convents, and important houses to prevent pillaging and outrage. Prisoners of war numbered only 550 sailors, 342 soldiers, and 25 officers. These were all French and members of the garrison proper. The 942 militiamen, considered as Canadians, were allowed to go back to their homes after having laid down their arms. As the English army entered the city, Townsend's soldiers commenced to distribute biscuits to all the hungry, sick and wounded. The day following, both English and Canadians set to work to reconstruct the five hundred ruined houses. As it was already the middle of September cold weather was close at hand, and adequate housing for the winter had to be assured.

At the end of a month the English fleet was ready to sail. On October 18 it left, some ships for England, and others for the American colonies with three companies of Louisbourg Grenadiers and five companies of Fusiliers; 7,313 English officers and men remained to garrison the city. In charge of administration was James Murray, whom Amherst had named as provisional governor.

For the first time since 1632, when the Kirkes restored Quebec to the French, the Canadians no longer had any relations with France. Now they had English rulers and military rulers at that. The force of occupation was, moreover, a mixed bag, since the English army was composed of Englishmen, New Englanders, some Germans, and even a few Jews who were in the Army's commissariat.

Canadians and English collaborated in the reconstruction of buildings, and in the care of sick and wounded. Under the influence of this co-operation the prejudices of both sides dissolved. The English learned to understand better the real differences between Frenchmen and Canadians. The Canadians on their part learned to distinguish between Englishmen and Colonials. It was out of this last difference that sprang most of the conflicts which later arose.

Marcel Trudel, *Le Régime Militaire dans le Gouvernement des Trois-Rivières, 1760-1764*, (Trois-Rivières, Editions du Bien Public, 1952), pp. 207-213. (Translated C.N.) Printed by permission of the author.

The Military Regime:

Highly Laudable

We have seen the functioning of the military regime in one of the three Governments of Canada. This military regime well deserves its name: the whole of the Government, for four years, was under the control of the English army; the Governor was a high army officer, and it is by military might that he administered the region; the Secretary of the Government was also an army officer: he was *Deputy Judge Advocate*, that is to say, secretary of the military court, and it was as such that he appended his signature when he examined the civil registers; it is the army treasury that supported the costs of administration; the captains of the militia, as they did elsewhere under the French regime, were the intermediaries between the superior authorities and the people, they saw to the execution of orders and the assignment of the *corvées*. The whole of the administration of justice depended on the militia and the army. . . . Even industry, that of the Saint-Maurice forges, was under the im-

mediate control of the military authority, and the profits were applied to the general administration under the same heading as the army funds. This regime was thus truly a military regime and could not be otherwise . . .

But, because this regime bears the name of a military regime, one might be tempted to consider it an oppressive regime. Our minute examination of the Government of Three Rivers does not, in general, warrant us to cry out against its oppression. Governor Burton was an English-speaking soldier, but he was associated with a bilingual secretary of Huguenot origin, who published all the notices in French and even signed his name *à la française,* Jean Bruyère. When he departed from Three Rivers he was replaced by a French-speaking Swiss, Conrad Gugy. When Burton replaced Gage at Montreal, his successor was Haldimand, a French-speaking Swiss . . . The notaries of the French regime were recognized by the military regime and the contracts they drafted were based on the Custom of Paris . . . We know that at least once Haldimand convened an assembly of bourgeois (as was done during the French regime) before establishing a new market place . . . One can say that in many cases it was an extension of the French regime.

Seen in this light, the military regime of the Government of Three Rivers seems to us a highly laudable regime, and it appears to merit even more eulogies if we recall a few extraordinary measures which were advantageous to the TriFluvians: the governors went to the trouble of having the Forges exploited to increase the circulation of currency, though no article of the Treaty required them to do so, nor to maintain the families located on the site. . . . Instead of calling up the militia for the campaign of 1764, the military regime turned to voluntary enlistments so that it might abide by the conditions of the Treaty of Paris. . . . Finally, the active part taken by the military authorities in the registering of paper money, the promise that England forced on the King of France to recognize this paper money, and the efforts made to obtain a prompt settlement of the matter, must have gained the sympathy of the Canadians. It was France, in this instance, that became unpopular . . .

This military regime, however, was not perfect, and as we draw up the balance sheet of its good works we must not forget the resentment of the TriFluvians towards it. After taking the oath of loyalty (an oath in no way vexatious), the inhabitants had to give up their arms: what was merely a measure of simple prudence on the part of the English may have made the population indignant. . . . It must be recognized, all the same, that this giving up of arms had its alleviation: they [the English] permitted each parish in the Government to retain a certain number of hunting guns, taking care that these weapons went to the people who most needed them. There is also the garrison for whose lodging the inhabitants were made responsible: even though the French regime had familiarized them with wartime billeting, one can be certain that the presence among them of English soldiers, inveterate enemies, made them detest the military regime; the lodging of the troops, however, was restricted . . . [and] we should add that the inhabitants who had to provide billets received rations from the army, and that the *corvées* of wood, hay and carriage seemed, on the whole, light. . . . The *habitant* wrote nothing, he has not left us any impressions, but, proud as he was, one can be certain he did not

easily bear the immediate presence of the conqueror.

Also, as it happened, this military regime caused discontent among the TriFluvial clergy. Certainly, till 1762, the relations between the Church and the English authorities continued good. . . . As soon as Canada belonged definitely to England, the relations between the Church and Burton immediately lost their cordiality. . . . Finally, Burton's insistence on two *Te Deums*, one to celebrate the signing of the Treaty of Paris and the other to celebrate its ratification, does not seem to us altogether without a certain malignity. If it is true, as Haldimand reports, that the clergy openly manifested its sympathies for France, and that it never ceased predicting success for the armies of Louis XV, one can perhaps understand Burton. . . .

The historian Garneau has written of this regime: "The military regime was a violation of the capitulations . . . Nothing contributed more to isolating the government from the population. . . ." This judgment astounds us by its great severity. Garneau does not seem to have understood that England absolutely could not grant the Canadians the rights of English subjects while the Canadians remained subjects of France [and] as long as a definitive treaty had not settled their fate. . . .

Apart from a few isolated cases . . . we cannot see how the military regime in Three Rivers could be styled as "the most insupportable tyranny." We are certain of this as regards the Government of Three Rivers, and we can be sure of it in advance for the Government of Montreal, where Burton and Haldimand worked hard to imitate the administration; and what we know of the Government of Quebec, even though there were more complaints of all kinds than elsewhere, permits us to affirm that Murray's administration was not a tyranny. The military regime, because of the very name, bears a bad reputation, but, in a country that did not definitely belong to it, England could only set up a provisional rule: elementary prudence obliged it to place the regime under the control of the army. It was a military regime, but not an arbitrary one, and the authorities carefully observed all the articles of the two capitulations.

All that Garneau wrote of the wrongs of the military regime he could have applied with equal precision to the inauguration of civil government. The social upheaval of which he speaks, the abolition of French laws, the arbitrariness —all these are produced after the 10th of August, 1764. . . .

R. H. Mahon, *Life of General the Hon. James Murray: a Builder of Canada,* (London, John Murray, 1921), pp. 28-321. Reprinted by permission of John Murray (Publishers) Ltd., London.

Murray, The Good

Governor?

Murray returned to Quebec about September 20, 1760. It is more than probable that a good many things had occurred which brought to him a feeling that he had received something less than a just consideration of his efforts. Amherst's despatch on the Montreal operations, in its reference to the part taken by the subordinate officers, was certainly brevity itself, and it scarcely conformed to Murray's own habit of giving generous acknowledgment to the action of others: "I should not do justice to Governor Murray and Colonel Haviland if I did not assure you they have executed the orders I gave them to the utmost of my wishes" (Amherst Despatch to Pitt, dated September 8, 1760).

If Murray was too loyal and too proud to say anything on the subject, he could hardly avoid reflecting that his men and himself had met with less than their due share of mention.

But not less galling was the inevitable criticisms of the newswriters, which began to filter through in open comments and inuendoes. The armchair critic of to-day is a mild and comparatively harmless individual compared with the mud-slinger of those days of unbridled anonymous license, when any name could be dragged through the dirt, if only the initial letters and a few asterisks were used to form a disguise which every one could see through; when a person who had failed in business was described as a "bxxkxxpt," to avoid any chance of libel! . . .

The Grub Street fraternity were unlikely to lose a chance of sharpening their wits on the operations of the previous April, and men, whose nearest approach to active service was to bolt from an attachment bailiff, were quite prepared to criticise the action of those who had faced hardships and dangers of which they had no conception. But, quite apart from mere Grub Streeters, there were others, higher placed, who did not scruple to condemn what they did not understand; and it must be remembered that the Whigs were not likely to lose an opportunity of having a stab at Lord Elibank's brother. Horace Walpole wrote of "General Murray, who got into a mistake and a morass, attacked two bodies that were joined where he hopes to come up with one of them before the junction, was enclosed, embogged, and defeated." But Walpole would no doubt have shone less as a leader than as a letter writer.

There was, besides, not a little evidence that there was a traitor from within the camp itself, who did not scruple to launch into anonymous attacks on superiors, as witness the scurrilous pamphlet which attempted to impute to Townshend much that he certainly was innocent of having done.

Even Townshend himself, who had left Quebec with the full intention of clearing up the dark places, had failed to come forward, and had probably found quite as much to do as he wanted in repelling attacks made on himself. He had, however, made in public some cryptic remarks on Murray's siege, which did not tend to make the latter feel good-tempered.

There was also a considerable current of opinion in England, which had probably by now reached Murray, that belittled the importance of the conquest of Canada, and urged its restoration at the peace, which was even then passed over—"that they had not the honour to serve with you in the last two campaigns, and it may prove unhappy for the officers in this garrison that their destination is still at so great a distance from you." Which was pretty straight talk!

He reserved for his brother George, however, a more complete unbosoming of his feelings. Frankly, it is not a letter I like quoting, and it exhibits traits which were not natural to the writer. It reminds me again of Wolfe, to whom, as I have said, Murray's character bore resemblance, and more than one of whose sentiments, written or spoken, cannot be said to conform with his true character.

The letter was in reply to one from George, dated July 12, which has already been quoted, and is dated October 19, 1760.

"You seem nettled," he wrote, "at the silence of the news writers, but if you'll cooly consider, I am highly honoured thereof.

"Mr. Townshend, Monckton, etc., etc., were in the right, perhaps, to hire these miscreants to relate feats they never performed, and to ascribe to themselves the actions of other men. I don't want any such trappings; it is praise of my brother soldiers I am ambitious of. I have the satisfaction to know my conduct has the approval of His Majesty and the Minister. . . . It will no doubt be known hereafter to all the world who opposed the attack of the lines of Montmorency, *and who in the beginning and to the very last of the campaign urged descent above the town at the very place where it was made,* and surely nobody is ignorant of what the left wing of the army did on September 13; *it* was not *'en potence,'* it broke the enemy's line and pursued the fugitives to the gates, and would have completed the destruction had it not been called off by superior authority.

"I fought a battle; I lost it. What then? Is every day of battle a day of victory? Did it be asked of any soldier if, in my situation, it was right to fight? He will answer without hesitation, 'To be sure!' Examine the disposition, compare it with the ground which must determine the propriety of it, and I flatter myself it will be allowed a good one. Was not the critical moment of attack made use of? Did it succeed? Was not the victory gained, had the right wing been as active and vigorous April 28, 1760, as the left wing was September 13, 1759? Was not aid instantly given during the action where it was wanted? Were not the cannon judiciously placed? Does not all this denote a presence of mind and a coupd'oile? (*sic*). Where was the General in this battle? Betwixt his own line and that of the enemy— everywhere where the enemy made a push animating his men by his presence. He had two horses shot under him, and his clothes riddled by the enemy's musketry. Where was he when the right wing faulter'd? He was placing the cannon on the heights in the centre, but rode instantly to the right, and there recovered the confusion. How did the troops retreat into town? In tolerable order, by means of the corps the General himself posted in the two unfinished redoubts, and on an eminence. Did he stay with the corps himself to the last? He did; he was the last man that enter'd the gates.

"The defence of the place, as it was successful, in England (where everything is right or wrong agreeable to the decision of Dame Fortune) will answer for itself. You are to ask the French generals what share had this campaign in the total reduction of Canada. I am persuaded Mr. Amherst is too just to be silent on that head. He certainly has told that I left him nothing to do, and that the Marquis de Vaudreuil insinuated terms of surrender to me, before Mr. Amherst's army appear'd, which I would not listen to, as I had intelligence of the commander-in-chief's being within six days' march of me, and I was posted at Longviel, by which the junction of the three armys (*sic*) was infallible.

"This much I have open'd myself to my brother. It is very wrong for a man to speak of himself, but he that praises himself is unpardonable. I therefore conjure you not to show this letter to anybody but Elibank. He and you may make what use of the contents you please, provided you do not let it be known that I have trumpeted my own fame.

"I think myself accountable to my family in a very particular manner for my actions, especially as the sphere I have lately acted in has been eminent. It will be your business to dive into the truth of every sentence of this letter, but not to expose me to the reproach of vain glory. I offer my very affectionate compliments to all my relations round you, and am, my dear George," etc.

With that part of his letter in which he unbared his soul regarding the action of April, for the private information of his family, I have no quarrel. It was natural that he should put his relations in possession of the part he had taken, and inform them of the inaccuracy of the insidious statements which had appeared in print; but I can only account for his bitterness regarding Townshend and Monckton, with both of whom he was on friendly terms, from the jaundiced view of the world which, at the moment, had possession of his mind, and from the fact that these officers, and many others, had left him with very inadequate resources to bear the brunt of the trouble-filled winter of 1759-60. The statement which I have printed in italics is, however, one which I cannot reconcile with other evidence. . . .

In the chapters which follow concerning the commencement of British Government in Canada, I aim at tracing its evolution from the terms of the capitulation at Montreal to the passing of the Quebec Act some fourteen years later. For much of the failure and confusion during these years General Murray has received unmerited censure, but I hope to make it clear that his efforts were thwarted and rendered ineffective by the same inept administrators who caused the loss of the American colonies. This latter subject has little to do with this volume, but it will be of interest to show how the neglect of the principles of common sense and even common honesty regarding Canada had their reflections in the treatment of the settled colonies.

In a recently published work Murray is accused of having unreasonably refused to call together an elected assembly in Quebec; of having treated the British traders with contempt; by some complex process of reasoning he is even accused of giving a "main and immediate cause to the revolutionary war," by *not* bringing this same assembly of British traders into being! Yet in the same work we are told that but for Murray these British traders would have had free rein for their evil natures to oppress the Canadians. Diversity of opinion such as this may well make the general reader wonder what is the truth, and this I hope to show by such references to the letters and other documents of the period as will enable judgment to be given.

The arrangements for the government of Canada made by Amherst pending formal orders from England were to maintain the separate Governments of Three Rivers and Montreal distinct from that of Quebec, as had been the case under the French regime. The first-named was placed in charge of Colonel Burton, who had been Murray's second in command; the Montreal province being handed to Brig.-Gen. Gage. Of the former, it may be said *en passant* that Murray had a high opinion. "I really have a friendship for him," he wrote to Amherst a little later.

The French civil officers were discharged—a measure which was probably instigated by the notorious want of honesty with which at that time they conducted their duties. Amherst ordained that government by martial law should replace the civil law until such time as the King's pleasure should be notified. . . .

His [Murray's] appointment as governor was in itself a tribute to his successes and the high character he had won for himself, but it was not accomplished without a considerable opposition. In the early days of discussion on the terms of the peace of Paris the idea of governing Canada had greatly attracted John Wilkes, and, through his intimacy with Lord Temple, who became Pitt's brother-in-law, he had obtained flattering assurances from the minister. The King, however, who liked to govern for himself, and had little affection at the time for Pitt, and none at all for Wilkes, it is said vetoed this proposal out of hand, and declared that the man who had defended Quebec was the one he wished to govern it. Wilkes' disappointment found utterance in the *North Briton* a couple of years later, and Murray did not escape his venomous pen. To be a Scot was in itself sufficient to incur the wrath of many of the political pamphleteers of the period, and Bute's rise to power as the King's confidential adviser made their bitterness fairly run over. The colonies were described as:

"Prey to the rapacity of four hungry Scottish governors† . . . as to the merits of three of these gentlemen I am a perfect stranger; the demerit of the Governor of Quebec the world has seen, for he nearly lost the most important conquest made during the whole war—a conquest purchased with the blood of one of our first heroes, the immortal Wolfe. Among a variety of new measures which this nation must ever deplore the appointment of military men to civil governments is not the least to be lamented. . . . I will only further observe on this head that the partiality of these appointments to every new Government we have acquired plainly marks the same hand so fatal and hostile to England. . . . A gazette so late as that of Saturday, October 8 (1763) must convince every man that even now that Scottish influence is not at an end, and that all pretences of that kind whether they are made by men in or out of power, are captious and delusive."

The "hand hostile to England," referred to Bute, and the gazette was that which contained Murray's appointment to Quebec. The Governor, however, does not seem to have been seriously disturbed by Wilkes' vituperation; indeed, the only reference I can find to him in the correspondence relates to the quality of the Highlanders who were anathema to men of Wilkes' kidney:

"Wilkes may say what he will, but every one must allow that Sandy is a good soldier, and always to be depended on. The debauched English soldier says Sandy has no more virtue than himself, for if his vice is drunkenness, Sandy's is avarice, which I am sorry to tell you, is not true, for they

†The other three were James Grant, Governor of East Florida; George Johnston, Governor of West Florida; and Robert Melvill, Governor of Granada, etc. Johnston was Murray's nephew, and his eccentricity made him notorious.

have spent all their money in ribbons for the Canadian girls! . . ."

It would appear that when he was still in uncertainty as to the fate of Canada, he had visions of retiring to a home life in Sussex, and it was no doubt with this idea uppermost that he purchased the estate of Denham, or Denham's Folly. This purchase is alluded to in a letter from Gideon Murray, dated April, 1762, so that the date is approximately fixed. Denham was apparently immediately re-christened *Beauport*, after the French village, near Quebec, which Murray had cause to know so well. In a letter dated September, 1763, Gideon Murray hints at a change in his brother's views. Referring to the transfer of certain moneys he says:

"For your American purchases, I heartily wish you joy and good success. As you are now Governor of Canada, your money will be best laid out there. Your Excellency must be a seignior; but I hope in time you'll transfer all and purchase in Britain, where it is more secure and less precarious in all respects. You must not therefore part with Beauport, but make it as you have designed it in due time, and if you do not chuse an absolute retirement, you may easily be chose Member for the Cinque Port."

In the early part of the year Murray had written to Mr. John Cranston, who was acting as his agent in Sussex:

"As there is now no doubt of a peace, and very little probability of my government being taken from me, I have no thought of visiting England. Indeed, I had some time ago determined to settle in America, whatever might be the consequences of a peace. I like the climate, and shall certainly never leave it unless the King's service obliges me. With this view my affairs are to be managed. . . . I wrote to your father to put a stop to all improvements proposed for Denham's

Folly, and to lay no more of my money out in Sussex."

In July of same year (1763) he wrote again concerning some money affairs: "You will see I am unalterably fix'd in this American world, and that I shall as soon as possible convert into it every shilling of property I have in the earth."

This was a somewhat sudden and a very complete change of mind. It was formed before the troubles of the quasi-civil government began to mount up, and perhaps Murray was enamoured of the idea of becoming a great landed proprietor in the New World; in this intention, I gather from another letter to Lord Elibank, his brother was apparently a partner, and some part of the money which was laid out in purchase of land in Canada was provided, or perhaps advanced, by his lordship. That he intended to go to work systematically to improve the land and farm on scientific principles is made clear from correspondence with his brother George, who was sending him two ploughmen, two milkmaids, and a grieve (farm bailiff), together with seeds and a good deal of advice as to the best methods of agriculture, in which George appears to have possessed quite a store of knowledge.

It was not, however, the prospect of farming on a large scale which alone attracted him to forego the dream of a retirement to country pursuits in Sussex; it is evident that he was thoroughly disgusted with the state of things in England, and the scant generosity with which he had been treated. The key to his feelings is given in a letter to George Murray, written in September, 1764:

"I have of late met with so much ingratitude and harsh treatment from those whose friendship, or at least goodwill, I thought I had a right to expect, that I am determined to settle for the remainder of my days in this New World. . . . I have no natural claims to the affection and gratitude of my neighbours. If they are defective in making returns for the benevolence which I make a duty of showing to all mankind, the disappointment will not be so shocking and irksome as if it proceeded from those in whom I have a nearer concern. Besides, I really find the aborigines of the country— or savages, as you style them—less corrupt in general than the inhabitants of the most civilised nations. They lend without interest; if a friend is lucky and kills more game, they envy him not, they rejoice at his success; if in war fortune has favoured him, they constantly ascribe his success to his military talents, and vie with one another in singing his praises. Envy and detraction are vices they are strangers to, nor do I think them near so cruel as their more refined neighbours, now settled among them. If they dislike a man they declare their hatred, and will not fail openly to attack their adversary when an opportunity offers, but the only weapons they make use of are martial arms; detraction and abuse they never practice, consequently they cannot be accused of cruel, cowardly assassinations of character. I tell you all this in vindication of the choice I have made; without an explanation it no doubt must have appeared more strange than at present I flatter myself it does. . . ."

Impartially viewed, I cannot but conclude that the strife which commenced during this period was not caused by Murray, who on every occasion surrendered his powers to preserve harmony; and even after he became aware that Burton had endeavoured to supplant him in the office of Governor, he was careful to avoid any reproach. Yet, as time passed, the action of the brigadier gradually exceeded all bounds of endurance, and finally culminated in a series of acts which were evidently calculated to produce an explosion. A certain Lieut.-Colonel Christie, who had been an officer in Amherst's Army, and was now deputy quarter-master-general under Burton, appears to have been the firebrand. Murray shrewdly suspected this officer of manipulating public affairs to his own benefit, and when a general warrant was applied for by Burton to enable him to impress boatmen and transport for military purposes, the Governor refused to grant it. Writing to General Gage (July 1, 1765) he says that Colonel Christie had already made improper use of such warrants, "And that gentleman is carrying on works to a very great extent for his own private emolument. Prudence will prevent me from giving him a general press warrant, and decency should hinder him from asking it." By October, 1765, the correspondence with Burton, now promoted to be major-general, had lost its old style of friendly intimacy. . . .

Part III

Civil

Government

After the Conquest the first civil government of Quebec was established by the Royal Proclamation of 1763. It became effective in 1764. The Captain General and Governor in Chief of this *Civil Government* was a military officer, James Murray. He had been a member of the conquering army and, as we have seen, the military governor of the City of Quebec. Murray's views were authoritarian, the heritage of his upbringing and occupation. A fundamental problem of the Proclamation, then, is the extent to which it represents the introduction of Civil Government.

Other aspects of the Proclamation have led to differences of opinion. William Smith, (1769-1847), was a member of the Executive Council of Lower Canada from 1817 to 1837. The son of the famous jurist of the same name, he is credited with writing one of the first comprehensive histories of Canada. Smith was a not too distant witness of the policies of the Military regime and the first Civil Government of Quebec. In his opinion the Proclamation had a decided purpose: the implementation of the British system of government and law in the colony of Quebec. In this Chester Martin concurs. Further, in opposition to W. S. Wallace, Martin claims it was a well-thought out piece of legislation. To Wallace the Proclamation was hastily conceived, and in no way met, or solved, the problems facing Quebec at that time. The Proclamation was a failure, at least in terms of its application. This has led historians to claim that the measure, like the military regime, was a transitory constitutional stage bridging the conquest of 1759-1760 and the Quebec Act which would follow in 1774.

Regardless of whether Smith, Wallace or Martin is right or wrong, this initial government of Quebec reveals both the British concept of their conquest, and the treatment to be meted out to the conquered. According to the letter of the law, the French Canadians lost all their civil rights. Also, unless they were willing to renounce their Roman Catholic faith, they lost all political rights. Their Church, without a bishop at this time, was doomed to a very marginal existence. But in this perspective, the intent of the Proclamation assumes a greater importance: if it meant what it said, it was tyrannical. If it was a minor oversight based on understandable ignorance, then indeed, like Pangloss, we live in the best of all possible worlds.

Murray, the man responsible for implementing the Proclamation, refused to abide by its provisions. By so doing he added lustre to his halo, a lustre which shines brightly to this day. Kindness, sympathy and understanding of the French Canadians probably all played a part in shaping his conduct. Elizabeth Arthur, however, places an emphasis upon more practical matters: the solving of the day-to-day problems Murray faced as Governor. An important question must be considered when Murray is being evaluated: could he have done other than he did? Miss Arthur suggests that the French Party was really Murray's Party. A further question poses itself: was the French Party devoted to protecting the interests of the French Canadians? Or was the French Party, in its opposition to the so-called English Party, merely championing the interests of the governor's clique?

William Smith, *History of Canada From Its Discovery to the Year 1791*, Vol. 2, (Quebec, John Neilson, 1815), pp. 3-18.

The Simplified

Overview

On the twenty-first day of November, one thousand seven hundred and sixty-three, about six weeks after the publication of the aforesaid proclamation, His Majesty issued his commission of Captain General and Governor in Chief of the province of Quebec to Major General Murray, which was received by him, and published in the province in the month of August, one thousand seven hundred and sixty-four. This commission, and the instructions that accompanied it, seemed everywhere to pre-suppose that the laws of England were in force in the province, being full of allusions and references to those laws on a variety of different subjects, and did not contain the least intimation of a saving of any part of the laws and customs that prevailed there, in the time of the French government.

It seemed therefore, upon the whole, from the proclamation and commission, to have been His Majesty's intention, with respect to the said province of Quebec, to assimilate the laws and government of it to those of the other American colonies and provinces which were under

His Majesty's immediate government, and not to continue the municipal laws and customs by which the conquered people had heretofore been governed, any farther than as those laws might be necessary to the preservation of their property. And His Majesty's ministers appeared, at the time of passing those instruments, to have been of opinion, that, by the refusal of General Amherst to grant to the Canadians the continuance of their ancient laws and usages; and by the reference made in the fourth article of the definitive treaty of peace to the laws of Great Britain, as the measure of the indulgence intended to be shewn them with respect to the exercise of their religion, sufficient notice had been given to the conquered inhabitants of that province, that it was His Majesty's pleasure, that they should be governed for the future, according to the laws of England; and that the inhabitants, after being thus apprised of His Majesty's intention, had consented to be so governed, and had testified their said consent, by continuing to reside in the country, and taking the oath of allegiance to His Majesty, when they might have withdrawn themselves from the province, with all their effects, and the produce of the sale of their estates, within the eighteen months allowed by His Majesty in the treaty of peace, for that purpose.

In pursuance of this supposition that the laws of England had been introduced into the province, by the aforesaid proclamation and commission, Governor Murray and his Council, in the great ordinance dated on the seventeenth day of September, one thousand seven hundred and sixty-four, (passed at the commencement of the civil government of the province, for the establishment of courts of justice in it), directed the Chief Justice of the province, (who was to hold the superior court, or *Court of King's Bench*, established by that ordinance), to *determine all criminal and civil causes agreeable to the laws of England and the ordinances of the province*; and the judges of the inferior court, established by the said ordinance, (which was called the *court of Common Pleas*,) *to determine the matters before them agreeable to equity, having regard nevertheless to the laws of England, as far as the circumstances and situation of things would permit, until such time as proper ordinances for the information of the people could be established by the Governor and Council, agreeable to the laws of England*; with this just and prudent proviso, *"that the French laws and customs should be allowed and admitted in all causes in the said court between the natives of the said province, in which the cause of action arose before the first day of October, one thousand seven hundred and sixty-four."*

In consequence of these instruments of Government, all purporting to introduce the laws of England into the province of Quebec, those laws were generally understood to have been introduced into it, and consequently to be the rule and measure of all contracts and other civil engagements entered into by the inhabitants after the introduction of them, that is, after the establishment of the civil government of the province, or after the said first day of October, one thousand seven hundred and sixty-four. Thus were the laws of England supposed to have been introduced, until the revival of the French laws in matters of property and civil rights by the Quebec Act passed some years afterwards.

As General James Murray had been appointed Governor of the province, and had been empowered by a Royal Instruction to nominate a Council of eight members of his choice, with power to make laws and ordinances; he was sworn in as Governor this year, and the Council nominated by him, were:

William Gregory — Chief Justice, Paulus Emilius Irving, Hector Theophilus Cramahé, Samuel Holland, Adam Mabane, Thomas Dunn, Walter Murray, François Mounier.

Chester Martin, *Empire and Common-wealth,* (Oxford, Clarendon Press, 1929), pp. 95-99. Reprinted by permission of the Clarendon Press.

Pro-Proclamation

Quebec was to become part of the 'American empire'. The 60,000 inhabitants of the new province were to 'become subjects of the King' and fellow-subjects with more than forty times that number of British subjects already in America. Among the questions referred to the Board of Trade by the Secretary for the Southern Department was the query 'what Privileges are reserved to His Majesty's New Subjects by the Terms of their Capitulations' and 'how far it is expedient to retain, or depart from the Forms of Government which His Most Christian Majesty had established in those Colonies'. 'The free exercise of their religion' was guaranteed to the Canadians in the capitulation of Montreal, but it was made clear that 'the obligation of paying the tithes . . . will depend on the King's pleasure', while at the Treaty of Paris privileges in religion were granted only 'as far as the laws of Great Britain permit'. The French plenipotentiaries 'proposed to insert the Words *comme ci-devant,* in order that the Romish Religion should continue to be exercised in the same manner as under their Government', but they were 'plainly told that it would

be deceiving them to admit those Words'. The demand at the capitulation of Montreal that 'the French and Canadians shall continue to be governed according to the custom of Paris, and the Laws and Usages established for this country' was refused with the significant reply that 'They become subjects of the King'.

Thus while the present prescriptive rights of Canadians of French origin are not less sacred in the Dominion than treaty rights or fundamental law of other nations they are not to be found in the policy contemplated for Quebec in 1763. Despite three rapid changes of ministry the measures for the government of the new province were drafted by the Board of Trade after 'most serious Consideration'. The Board itself still bore the stamp of Halifax's brilliant reorganization of that much-maligned body, and Halifax himself was now in control at the Southern Department. John Pownall, the indefatigable Secretary of the Board, whose influence had sometimes been all-powerful during the Halifax régime, was now, after a brief leave of absence with Halifax in Ireland, back again at his old office. Hillsborough, another of Halifax's staff in Ireland, was at the head of the Board. It was under Halifax's own instructions of September 19, 1763, that the Board undertook to 'declare the Constitution of the new Governments, as established for the present, & intended in future'. 'The form', writes Dr. Alvord, 'was undoubtedly due to the influence of Pownall', and the final policy was 'due to Lord Halifax'. For Quebec as for Nova Scotia it is reasonable to suppose that Shirley's 'Great Plan' was again in the ascendant. In the early reports and correspondence of the Board, in the resulting Order in Council, in the Proclamation of October 7, 1763, issued by Halifax himself—the constitution of

Quebec until the *Quebec Act*—in the Commission to Governor Murray, in the elaborate Instructions which followed, in the Commission to Carleton as governor in 1768, in the *Report* of the Board of Trade in 1765, and above all in the incisive *Report* of 1769, next to the *Quebec Act* itself perhaps the most important document of the period in Canadian history, one searches in vain for any official departure from the recognized forms and functions of British colonial government in North America.

During the debates on the *Quebec Act* the attempt was made to attribute the policy of 1763 to haste and inadvertence. Evidence to the contrary is to be found in a score of documents of every degree of historical conclusiveness.

Prevailing conceptions in the mercantile system were of course taken for granted. The Board advised the 'secure settling' of the country either by European emigration 'or from the Overflowing of Your Majesty's ancient Colonies'. Among all the conquests of the Seven Years' War Canada was placed first among the 'Places where Planting, and perpetual Settlement and Cultivation ought to be encouraged and consequently where regular Forms of Government must immediately be established'. In the formal Instructions to Murray no fewer than sixteen sections relate to the 'advantageous and effectual Settlement' of the new province. The governor was instructed, no doubt with Lawrence's experience in Nova Scotia in mind, to invite British settlement by 'Proclamation in all the Colonies in North America.'

Nowhere was the incorporation of Quebec into the old colonial system more clearly foreshadowed than in the proposed form of government. Variations in

law and legal practice were of course taken for granted. Hillsborough afterwards stated that 'it never entered into Our Idea to overturn the Laws and Customs of Canada, with regard to Property', though justice was to be administered 'according to the Laws of England'. With regard to franchise and legal rights the law officers of the Crown decided from the outset that Roman Catholics were 'not subject, in those Colonies, to the Incapacities, disabilities, and Penalties, to which Roman Catholics in this Kingdom are subject by the Laws thereof'. In truth neither law nor religion was vitally related to the issues that were already overshadowing the whole problem of colonial government in America. Boundaries and Indian policy were more significant. But the form of government itself was fundamental. From the decision in Nova Scotia in 1756 to the great *Report* of 1769 there is no deviation here in the deliberate policy of the Board. In the end, as we shall see, their insistency was such that the whole problem of government for Quebec was summarily removed from their hands and dealt with as 'a matter of State Politics' at the most critical stage of the American Revolution.

Traditions of arbitrary governance in Quebec were not unknown either to the Board or to the American colonies. In 1754 Benjamin Franklin objected to Shirley's scheme of a Commander-in-Chief and Council for America because such a system 'would put them on a Footing with the Subjects of France in Canada. . . . If the Colonies in a Body may be well governed by Governors and Councils, appointed by the Crown, without Representatives, particular Colonies may as well or better be so governed.' It is true that Murray during the military occupation of Quebec had opposed an Assembly, but this was not the first record of a military governor's distaste for the 'heats, Animosities and disunion' usually associated with representative institutions. More than one indulgent member of the Board must have recalled the instructions to Governor Lawrence in Nova Scotia in 1758. Thus the Board of Trade, after nearly five months' deliberation and two preliminary reports, placed in the hands of Lord Halifax, who had himself presided over the Board in 1758, the instruments which formed the constitution of Quebec until the *Quebec Act*. And since it would 'give Confidence and Encouragement (they added), to such Persons as are inclined to become Settlers in the new Colonies, That an immediate and public Declaration should be made of the intended permanent Constitution and that the power of calling Assemblies should be inserted in the first Commissions, We have therefore drawn the Proclamation agreeable to this Opinion, and have prepared the Commissions accordingly'.

In Proclamation, Commission, and Instructions accordingly the 'intended permanent Constitution' is outlined in ascending degrees of incisiveness. The first of these, in the interests of 'speedy settling', established the normal type of 'royal' province:

'We have, in the Letters Patent under our Great Seal of Great Britain, by which the said Governments are constituted, given express Power and Direction to our Governors of our said Colonies respectively, that so soon as the state and circumstances of the said Colonies will admit thereof, they shall, with the Advice and Consent of the Members of our Council, summon and call General Assemblies . . . in such Manner and Form as is used and directed in those Colonies and Provinces in America which are under our immediate Government.'

Murray's Commission, drafted by the Board in complete accord with the Proclamation, contained the same provisions for a representative Assembly which had forced the summoning of the Nova Scotia Assembly in 1758. At the time of the *Quebec Act* the Advocate-General, James Marriott, suggested that these provisions were applied to Quebec, 'inadvertently, and in the hurry of office'. It is impossible to suppose that the Board of Trade which drafted them, or Lord Halifax who carried them into execution, could have been ignorant of the principles which both had been at such pains to enforce against Governor Lawrence's scruples in Nova Scotia. It had then been agreed that 'the Governor & Council alone are not Authorized . . . to make Laws', and that neither the governor's objections nor 'any other Reason can justify the Continuation of the Exercise of an illegal Authority'. The truth was, as Lord Mansfield stated in the case of *Campbell* v. *Hall* in 1774, that by the Proclamation and Commission 'the King had immediately and irrevocably granted' an Assembly 'in like manner as in the other provinces under the King'.

And finally the Instructions were perhaps the most insistent of all. Here alone the Board had provided for the necessary interval pending the summoning of an Assembly. The governor and council were expressly forbidden to pass any ordinance 'that shall any ways tend to affect the Life, Limb or Liberty of the Subject, or to the imposing any Duties or Taxes'; and since by his Commission the governor was to 'summon and call a General Assembly' he was to 'give all possible attention to the carrying this important Object into Execution'. No fewer than twelve paragraphs of the Instructions relate to 'tacking', to 'the sole framing of Money Bills', and to other tendencies of Assemblies in the 'royal' provinces. It came to pass that more than one ordinance of Murray and his council had to be disallowed 'from a consideration of the Want of a due authority to enact them'. As late as 1769 the Board was ready to stake its own existence upon the summoning of an Assembly 'for the establishment of which it is humbly conceived the Faith of the Crown stands fully pledged'.

W. S. Wallace, "The Beginnings of British Rule in Canada", *Canadian Historical Review*, Volume VI, 1925, pp. 208-221. Reprinted by permission of the University of Toronto Press and the Author.

Anti-Proclamation

. . . To most Europeans Canada was still, as it had been to Voltaire, "a few acres of snow". What decided the British statesmen in favour of the acquisition of Canada was their desire to remove the menace of French aggression from the English colonies to the south. They took Canada, not indeed to make use of it themselves, but to prevent the French from making use of it.

It was this attitude on the part of the British authorities which determined the character of the first provisions made for the civil government of the newly acquired territories. These were embodied in the Royal Proclamation of October 7, 1763, which was issued six months after the signing of the Peace of Paris, and was one of the most casual and inadequate instruments of government in the history of colonial rule. The original object of the proclamation was to afford protection to the Indians in the western country of North America, and to confine European settlement to the sea-board. The successor of King Cnut, [*sic*] in effect, bade the waves of the sea to recede. At a later stage, however, provisions were introduced into the proclamation dealing *en bloc* with the establishment of civil government in the four territories of Quebec, East and West Florida, and the island of Grenada. These provisions defined the boundaries of these several provinces, and, in one sweeping paragraph, prescribed for them one and all, without regard for any difference of circumstances, the same system of government and law.

The effect of the proclamation, so far as the province of Quebec was concerned, was to create a government out of what was nothing more than the settled part of New France. The boundaries of the new province were roughly the River St. John on the east, a line drawn from Lake St. John to Lake Nipissing on the north, a line drawn from Lake Nipissing to the intersection of the St. Lawrence by the forty-fifth parallel of latitude on the west, and the height of land between the St. Lawrence valley and the Atlantic on the south. The western country, with its chain of trading posts stretching to the prairies and the Mississippi valley, was left outside the pale of the province, under the supervision of the department of Indian affairs. Within the province, the executive government was placed in the hands of a governor and a council; and the governor was instructed that "so soon as the state and circumstances of the said colonies will admit thereof" he was to call a general assembly similar to the assemblies in the older English colonies to the south. Legislative power was placed in the hands of the governor, acting in conjunction with the council and the assembly. Whether, in the event of the assembly not being summoned, legislative power resided in the governor and council alone, was not made clear. The instructions to Murray directed him to make rules and regulations for the peace and good order

of the province, short of affecting "the Life, Limb or Liberty of the Subject". But the language of the proclamation did not seem to contemplate even this modest power; for the assurance was given, with smug Anglo-Saxon self-complacency, that "until such assemblies can be called as aforesaid, all persons inhabiting in or resorting to our said colonies may confide in our Royal protection for the enjoyment of the benefit of the laws of our realm of England". For this purpose, the governor, in conjunction with the council, was empowered to create courts of justice, in which all causes were to be determined, "as near as may be, agreeable to the laws of England". From these courts appeals were to lie to the Privy Council.

It is clear that those who drew up these provisions were sadly ignorant of conditions in Canada. The restrictions of the boundaries of the province completely ignored the fact that Canada still relied for its prosperity on the western fur-trade. To compel the merchants whose headquarters were at Quebec and Montreal to carry on their business in territories outside the province, where there was no adequate civil jurisdiction, was certain to prove unsatisfactory; and in 1774, largely as the result of representations from Canada, it was found necessary to include these territories in the province of Quebec. The proposal to summon an assembly failed to take into account the fact that the population of the province was composed of at least sixty-five thousand French-Canadian Roman Catholics, who under the laws of England were presumably debarred from sitting in the assembly, and only two or three hundred "old subjects", mostly traders who had come into the province in the wake of the army. To throw political power into the hands of the latter to the exclusion of the former would have been to set up a racial oligarchy. It is significant of the situation in Canada that a generation was to elapse before it was deemed possible to erect there representative institutions. As for the promise of English law, if it implied, as it seemed to imply, that the French law was to be abolished, the best that can be said for it is that it was impracticable. To attempt to interpret seigniorial tenure in the light of the English law of free and common socage, or even a French commercial contract in the light of the English contract law, presented insuperable difficulties. And in 1774 Chief Justice Hey confessed before the bar of the House of Commons that he had been compelled to "admit the French laws and customs indiscriminately, in general," in the court of king's bench.

The omissions in the proclamation were as remarkable as its ineptitudes. Not only were the governor and council left apparently without power of legislation, in the event of failure to call an assembly; but nothing was said about taxation. The English crown had presumably taken over from the French crown the duties which had been in force in Canada during the French régime; but whether the governor and council were empowered to collect even these duties, was left in uncertainty. Not until the Quebec Revenue Act of 1774 was taxation in Quebec placed upon a satisfactory footing. Equally unfortunate was the failure of the proclamation to define the status of the Roman Catholic Church. By the Peace of Paris, the king of England had agreed to "give the most precise and most effectual orders that his new Roman Catholic subjects may profess the worship of their religion, according to the rites of the Romish Church, as far as the laws of Great Britain permit". Just how far the laws of Great Britain

extended toleration to Roman Catholics in Canada, was the question. Roman Catholics in Great Britain and Ireland at this time were under severe disabilities; the Test and Toleration Acts were still technically in force. Did these Acts apply to Canada, or, if not, what restrictions were to be adopted in Canada? The royal instructions to Murray were that he was "not to admit of any Ecclesiastical Jurisdiction of the See of Rome". But these instructions were silent on a number of points, such as the admissibility of Roman Catholics to juries, to public office, or to commissions in the army, and the legal enforcement of the payment of tithes. The French commander had asked at the capitulation of Montreal in 1760 that the Canadians "shall be obliged by the English Government to pay to the priests . . . the tithes and all the dues they were accustomed to pay under the Government of his Most Christian Majesty"; and the British commander had replied that "the obligation of paying the tithes to the priests will depend on the King's pleasure." Not until 1774, however, was the King's pleasure made known.

The very validity of the proclamation was in time called into question. In 1766 Francis Maseres, on his appointment as attorney-general of Quebec, drew up, with the approval of the new lieutenant-governor, Carleton, and the new chief justice, Hey, a paper in which he argued that "the Parliament only have a power to make laws for the province of Quebec". It is true that the English colonies to the south owed their charters as a rule to royal, rather than to parliamentary, authority; but, as Maseres pointed out, most of these charters dated from the Stuart period. The validity of the proclamation was finally established by the judgment of Lord Mansfield in the case of Campbell *v.* Hall in 1774. This important judgment laid down the principle that a grant of legislative institutions, such as that made by the Royal Proclamation of 1763, was irrevocable. It is therefore a sort of Magna Carta of colonial liberties. Incidentally, it proceeded on the assumption that the Royal Proclamation of 1763 was a valid form of legislation; and it consequently had the effect of establishing the proclamation as the constitution of Quebec from 1763 to 1774. The fact, however, that during these years there was doubt as to the legality of the proclamation, was merely another illustration of its unsatisfactory character.

Civil government was set up in Quebec in the sumer of 1764. After Pitt had declined to be relegated to political obscurity *via* Canada, the governorship of the province of Quebec was conferred on Murray, who had been since 1759 the military governor of the district of Quebec. Lieutenant-governors were also appointed for the districts of Three Rivers and Montreal; but these offices were discontinued within a few months, and were never revived. A council of twelve members was formed, to be composed of the two lieutenant-governors, the chief justice, the surveyor-general, and eight others to be nominated by the governor. In this first council one French Canadian, a Protestant, was included. On September 17, 1764, Murray issued an ordinance setting up a system of justice and police. A court of king's bench, presided over by the chief justice, was instituted, to be a superior court for the province; and a court of common pleas, to be an inferior court for the use chiefly of the French Canadians. Justices of the peace were created; and provision was made for the holding of quarter-sessions in the districts

of Quebec and Montreal. Constables, or "bailiffs", were to be nominated by the governor from among a number elected by the inhabitants of each parish. In this ordinance Murray somewhat exceeded his instructions. He had been instructed by the king that, in creating a system of justice, he should "consider what has taken place in this respect in Our other Colonies in America, more particularly in Our Colony of Nova Scotia". When it is remembered that there had taken place in Nova Scotia only a few years before this a wholesale deportation of the Acadians, this reference to Nova Scotia assumes a somewhat sinister aspect. Murray chose to ignore his instructions in this regard, and to introduce into the ordinance on his own authority some provisions of a very different tenor. In the court of king's bench, he admitted as jurors "all His Majesty's Subjects in this Colony . . . without Distinction"; and in the court of common pleas he permitted French-Canadian advocates to practise, and he ordained that the French laws and customs were to be allowed in all causes between natives of the province, where the cause of action arose before October 1, 1764. He thus took the first step in the process which led to the adoption of that policy of conciliation of the French Canadians which was embodied in the Quebec Act of 1774.

Indications are not lacking that the policy which the British government first purposed adopting in the case of Canada was one of repression of the French Canadians. The Royal Proclamation of 1763, with its apparent abolition of the French laws, suggests as much. Five years later, it is true, Lord Hillsborough, who had been in 1763 president of the Board of Trade and Plantations, which had oversight of the colonies, expressly denied that the framers of the proclamation had intended to abolish the whole of the French laws. "I can take it upon me to averr," he wrote, "that it never entered into Our Idea to overturn the Laws and Customs of Canada, with regard to Property, but that Justice should be administered agreeably to them, according to the Modes of administering Justice in the Courts of Judicature of this Kingdom, as is the Case in the County of Kent, and many other parts of England, where Gavel-kind Borough-English and several other particular customs prevail, altho' Justice is administered therein according to the Laws of England." But, plausible as this *ex post facto* statement may appear, the absence of any hint of such an intention either in the proclamation or in the governor's commission and instructions throws doubt on the accuracy of Lord Hillsborough's memory. In any case, a passage in Murray's instructions places the question of the attitude of the British government beyond peradventure. Murray was instructed to give all possible encouragement to the erection of Protestant schools among the French Canadians, and to provide for the maintenance of Protestant ministers and Protestant school-masters, "to the End that the Church of England may be established both in Principles and Practice, and that the said Inhabitants may by Degrees be induced to embrace the Protestant Religion, and their Children be brought up in the Principles of it". Thus, without any drastic Acadian expulsion, Canada was to become gradually a British Protestant colony, a newer New England.

Opposition to this Anglicizing policy manifested itself from the first. As soon as he learned of the tenor of the Royal Proclamation of 1763, Lord Mansfield wrote in vehement protest to George Grenville, who had succeeded Bute as prime minister. "The history of the world don't furnish an instance of so rash and unjust an act by any conqueror whatsoever." In the autumn of 1764, an address of the French inhabitants in Canada was forwarded to the king, praying for the confirmation of the concessions granted to them by Murray in his ordinance of September 17. And Murray himself was unremitting in his endeavours to secure a more generous treatment of the French Canadians. Writing to the Board of Trade, he described them as "perhaps the best and the bravest race upon the Globe, a Race who cou'd they be indulged with a few priveledges which the Laws of England deny to Roman Catholicks at home, would soon get the better of every National Antipathy to their Conquerors and become the most useful and most faithful set of Men in this American Empire". If the penal laws against Roman Catholics were to be enforced in Canada, he asked that his resignation should be accepted. Carleton, who succeeded Murray in the government of Quebec, took up similar ground. The abolition of French law he characterized as "A Sort of Severity, if I remember right, never before practiced by any Conqueror, even where the people, without Capitulation, submitted to His Will and Discretion". Carleton saw no future before Canada but as a French province of Great Britain. "Barring Catastrophe shocking to think of," he wrote to Shelburne in 1767, "this Country must, to the end of Time, be peopled by the Canadian Race." It seemed to him essential, therefore, that the French Canadians should be attached to the British crown by means of every possible concession. Carleton, indeed, went so far as to advocate the inclusion of members of the French Canadian *noblesse* in the council and their admission to commissions in the army.

The result of this opposition was the gradual abandonment of the policy of 1763. As early as the autumn of 1764, an additional instruction was sent to Murray, to the effect that the Royal Proclamation of 1763 should not operate "to take away from the native Inhabitants the Benefit of their own Laws and Customs in Cases where Titles to Land, and the modes of Descent, Alienation and Settlement are in Question, nor to preclude them from that share in the Administration of Judicature, which both in Reason and Justice they are intitled to in Common with the rest of our subjects". These instructions were put into effect by an ordinance dated July 1, 1766, which permitted French-Canadian jurors to sit, and French-Canadian lawyers to plead, in any court in the colony; and by an ordinance of 1767, which confirmed to the French-Canadians their land laws. In 1766, moreover, an important concession was made to the Roman Catholic Church. The last French bishop of Quebec had died shortly after the conquest; and, in view of the attitude of the British government, a successor had not been consecrated. Now, largely owing to the efforts of Cramahé, a councillor whom Murray had sent to London to press his views upon the government, an informal permission was given by the British authorities for the consecration of a bishop; and in the summer of 1766 Mgr. Briand was consecrated in France bishop of Quebec. It appears, indeed, to have been understood that he would adopt in Canada the title of superintendent of the Roman Catholic Church; but, as a matter of fact, he assumed, on his return to Canada, the full style and position of bishop.

By one party in Canada the abandonment of the policy of 1763 was viewed with alarm and disgust. This was the English mercantile, as distinct from the military, element in the colony. The character of this element has always been painted in dark colours. Murray, with his caustic pen, described them as "four hundred and fifty contemptible sutlers and traders"; and even the more moderate Carleton classed them as "either disbanded Officers, Soldiers, or Followers of the Army, who, not knowing how to dispose of themselves elsewhere, settled where they were left at the Reduction; or else they are Adventurers in Trade, or such as could not remain at Home". There were among them, however, men of ability and integrity, who afterwards rose to positions of importance in the colony. Nor were their views wholly unreasonable. They had come into the province on the strength of the promise contained in the Royal Proclamation of 1763 that English laws and English institutions would prevail there; and they demanded that the British government should not break faith with them. The failure of the governor to call an assembly became at an early date a grievance in their eyes; and when they saw inroads being made on the other features of the proclamation, their indignation knew no bounds. . . .

Unfortunately, the constitutional struggle between the governor and the merchants was embittered by other factors. Between them there was a wide gulf fixed in social standing and in political ideals. The governor and his entourage felt toward the merchants the contempt entertained by the English gentleman of the eighteenth century for all who were engaged in trade. Similarly, their aristocratic principles were in direct conflict with the advanced democratic ideas of the merchants, who were chiefly Scotch radicals or New England colonists. The situation was further complicated by the feud between the English merchants and the military, with whom the governor and his set were suspected of being in sympathy. Murray himself had confessed that he did not expect peace in the colony until the officers and soldiers "who have governed this Country for five years before the Establishment of Civil Government are entirely removed". The failure of the government, however, to bring to justice the soldiers who assaulted Thomas Walker, and cut off his ear, on the evening of December 6, 1764, at Montreal, created the impression that the governor could not be relied upon to protect the merchants against the military. The Walker affair, indeed, almost divided the colony into armed camps; and it had far-reaching results in the political sphere.

The dissensions in the province, which could be traced in no small measure to the unfortunate terms of the Royal Proclamation of 1763, early directed the attention of the British government to the necessity for more satisfactory arrangements. As early as 1765 the question of the status of Roman Catholics in Canada was referred to the British attorney-general and solicitor-general; and these officers reported that, in their opinion, Roman Catholics in Canada were not subject to the disabilities under which Roman Catholics in Great Britain laboured. On the basis apparently of this opinion, the Board of Trade recommended a few months later that an assembly should be called in Quebec, the representatives to be Protestants, but the voters both Protestants and Roman Catholics. In 1766 the question of the administration of justice in Quebec was referred to the attorney-

general and the solicitor-general; and they reported in favour of a mixed system of French and English civil law. No action was taken on this report, however, owing to one of those sudden changes in the administration which were at this time almost an annual feature of English politics. . . .

The government of Quebec from 1764 to 1774 was not one of the bright spots of British colonial rule in the eighteenth century. On nearly every point of constitutional importance there was during this period grave uncertainty. The governor did not know whether he had the power of collecting even the taxes levied during the French régime; the British merchants did not know whether they would or would not be granted an assembly; the seigniors were in doubt as to whether their seigniorial rights were to be continued to them; the Roman Catholic Church was in the dark as to its status; and the *habitants* were mystified about everything. To determine, for example, just what body of law was in actual force in Canada during this period would have taxed the ingenuity of the most subtle jurist. There was doubt even as to the constitution of the council. There were two classes of members in the council, those who had been appointed under the royal instructions to Murray, and those who had been appointed by *mandamus* from the king. The question arose as to which of these had precedence, particularly in the event of the council becoming over strength; and Carleton came to a serious disagreement with Murray's appointees on the council over this point. Nor were these defects counterbalanced by even a reasonable degree of efficiency in the executive government. Murray and Carleton were both able and upright men;

and Hey, who was chief justice after 1766, discharged the duties of his office with singular tact and good judgment. But Gregory, the first chief justice, and Suckling, the first attorney-general, understood neither English law nor the French language, and were poor and rapacious into the bargain. So unsatisfactory were the justices of the peace appointed under the ordinance of 1764 that in 1770 Carleton was obliged to issue an ordinance seriously curtailing their powers. A real abuse, moreover, existed in the system of fees, by which every official in the colony supplemented his salary. Carleton, on assuming office in 1766, issued a proclamation relinquishing the fees attaching [*sic*] to his own office, and he strove repeatedly to have the system abolished; but he was unsuccessful, and the system persisted for many years later. A curious outgrowth of the system was the practice of permitting officials to appoint deputies. In 1764, for instance, Henry Ellis, who had been since 1761 absentee governor of Nova Scotia, was appointed "clerk of the council, secretary of the province, registrar of the inrollments, and steward or commissary-general of the provisions and stores" for Quebec, with power to appoint deputies. Ellis drew in England the salaries for this rather remarkable conglomeration of offices; and he appointed deputies who came to Quebec, and who apparently made a good living out of the fees. Nor was Ellis's an isolated case. For nearly half a century absentee officials were a familiar feature of Canadian government. . . .

Elizabeth Arthur, *Adam Mabane and the French Party in Canada,* (Montreal, McGill University, 1947), (unpublished M.A. thesis), pp. 35-40, 49-51. Reprinted by permission of the Author.

Murray's Family Compact:

The French Party?

Although the French party in Canada had Adam Mabane as its leader throughout almost its entire existence, it owed its beginning rather to the first British Governor of the country, General James Murray. . . . Although Murray remained in Canada for less than two years after the civil government was established, his ideas became part of the basic philosophy of an important political group that continued long after his departure. In the midst of the violent quarrels that raged about him, the leading men in the country, following the example of their governor, were likely to become partisans; and the French party may thus, in its early days, be defined as the group that supported Murray. Expressing remarkably few opinions of their own, a small group of which Mabane was the most prominent, followed the governor through the years 1764-1766, accepting with him a new conception of the rôle of Britain in Canada, and shedding with him in large measure at least, the predilections for the English form of government, the English

laws, and even the English religion, with which they had come to the country.

Adam Mabane, it is true, was a conspicuous figure in Canadian public life during the Murray regime, for he was both a judge in the Court of Common Pleas, and a councillor; but his importance at that time consisted rather in his patient following of the governor's directions than in daring leadership of any party. Never an original thinker, and always apt to be swayed excessively by his own likes and dislikes, Mabane seems to have absorbed Murray's opinions and adopted Murray's enemies as his own. The governor, in his turn, had a high opinion of Mabane, even going so far as to praise his skill as a physician. Concerning this matter, Murray was scarcely competent to judge, and certainly his opinion seems to stand alone in this regard, but concerning Mabane's loyalty he made no mistake, and the friendship that grew up between the two was genuine and lasting. Mabane was sedulous in his attention to his new duties, almost invariably present at council meetings, acting as chairman of numerous committees which returned exhaustive reports, endeavouring to be fair in his judicial decisions and pleasing neither French nor English as a result, giving up his private practice that he might devote all his time to official business—yet he was still open to the charge of being a placeman. . . . In the 1760's, he held three official positions at one time: councillor, surgeon to the British garrison at Quebec, and judge; and for the last of these he had no training whatever—the only possible excuse for his appointment was that no one else in the colony had any better qualifications. His faithful service and his sacrifice of a lucrative practice for the uncertain rewards of office were not sufficient to shield him from the criticisms of the merchant group. He was much too closely identified with Murray to escape.

It is this identification of the party and the governor that makes it necessary to examine very closely the ideas Murray had formulated and the policies into which they led him. He had begun—as all the members of the French party began— with a vague feeling of sympathy for the distressed Canadians and a certain admiration for their docility. His observations during his first year in Canada had led him to certain conclusions which he expressed as early as October, 1760, in a letter to Pitt. He remarked upon the ignorance of the Canadian *habitant*, the influence of the clergy, and hinted at the next logical step in such an argument— using the clergy to win *habitant* support for the new regime. "I am endeavouring," he wrote, "to cultivate close connections with some in the hope of winning all."

By the time that he made his complete report on the state of Quebec in 1762, Murray's thinking had progressed much further, and for the first time he had concrete suggestions to offer. Instead of the descriptions of the destruction wrought by war, which appeared in his earlier despatches, there was the suggestion that tax burdens upon the Canadians should be extremely light, in order to allow them to rebuild their homes, and also as a method of securing their allegiance. This was obviously meant as a temporary policy, but the French party continued it long after the damages caused by the Seven Years' War had been repaired, and made it a permanent principle to oppose practically every public expenditure. Extravagant spending, to Mabane and his followers, meant the certain intervention of the British ministry, and very probably the creation of a house of assembly,

against which they fought a losing battle. Murray early declared his aims were to encourage industry and agriculture, but outside of attempts to improve his own seigneury, in which he took great interest, he concentrated his attention upon political matters. This concentration upon political considerations almost to the exclusion of economic, was a characteristic of the French party throughout its entire history. . . . The French party never developed positive or practical views on finance, as if the very absorption of their opponents in such matters made them unworthy of attention. . . .

During the same years, the relations between Murray and his friends on the one hand and the French seigneurs on the other underwent a similar and equally striking change. Murray's early impressions of the Canadian gentry were almost as harsh as any formed by the English merchants, for whose opinions Murray had such scant respect. He characterized the seigneurs as impecunious, haughty, tyrannical to their vassals, contemptuous of trade, and unalterably attached to French rule, as Britain could never offer them the position they had formerly enjoyed. The seigneurs themselves certainly had the impression that Murray was anxious for them to return to France, and some did avail themselves of the opportunity, though these were comparatively few in number. Partly because of genuine attachment to Canada, partly because, contrary to Murray's opinion, they felt their influence here would be greater than in France, partly because of their poverty, the majority of the gentry remained where they were.

By the time that he left Canada in 1766, Murray's attitude had changed considerably. Now it was not the tyranny of the feudal system that impressed him, but its orderly character, the healthy respect that tenants bore their lords, the nominal nature of the rents required. He even grouped his own nominees for office—the nucleus of the French party—with the seigneurs, when he spoke of the horror with which the *habitants* viewed "the insults which their noblesse and the King's officers have received from the English traders and lawyers."

Murray's enemies were not slow in pointing out this inconsistency, and in suggesting what was probably the correct explanation: that as soon as a rift appeared between the governor and the old subjects, he turned toward the noblesse for support. . . .

Part IV

The English Party
vs. Murray
the Tyrant

The English Party, in Canadian historical literature, has been cast in the rôle of a *heavy*, a Simon Legree-like group opposed to Murray, the French Canadians, and British *fair play*. Their chief demands were for their rights as British subjects, one of which was the calling of a representative assembly. Fortunately, it is written, their evil designs were thwarted, their ambitions were stifled, and justice was done the French Canadians. This racial struggle (?) between the so-called English Party and so-called French Party is thus an early manifestation of *bonne ententisme* and a striking example of the innate duality of the Canadian nation. Let us examine the matter further.

The French and English Parties were, on the whole, both made up of members of the conquering group. Murray's eight-man Council contained but one French Canadian. The English *establishment* included some French Canadians. Was the struggle a racial one? And did the relative defeat of the English Party's designs result in the dominance by the French Canadians of the economic and political spheres in Quebec?

The Old Subjects, that is the English citizens in Quebec, came to the newly conquered lands for commercial purposes. They had been invited to do so by the British military authorities. They accepted, with more or less grace, the Military regime as a temporary policy. The introduction of Civil Government appeared to them a realization of economic and political aims.

This "Merchant's Programme" is examined further by D. G. Creighton. The members of the English Party were the imperialists of the "Empire of the Saint Lawrence"; they deeply resented the curtailing of their political rights and, as important if not more so, the constriction of the boundaries of Quebec. This had, in effect, cut them off from the fur hinterland. They also believed, and partially correctly, that trade permits, controlled as they were by Governor Murray, tended to fall into too many hands other than their own.

The trade-and-politics crisis exploded over the lost hearing organ of Thomas Walker, a member of the English Party. Walker, apparently a less than amiable character, was having supper with his family and clerk one night. His house was invaded by a few members of the military establishment and, after a *fracas*, the English merchant found himself minus one ear. Walker was a member of the English Party, whose views follow. They were referred to by Murray as "The Licentious Fanaticks." This was the governor's gentle characterization of the group that opposed him and his party.

The Old Subjects complained, as did the New Subjects, that is, the conquered. Somehow the members of the English Party managed to hoodwink their French Canadian members into signing the "Presentment of the Grand Jury of Quebec." The French Canadians then were forced to disassociate themselves from the "Presentment", and they took the opportunity to remind the British government that they had loyally adapted themselves to their new rulers, but that their fellow citizens, the English, "make us feel our Condition to be that of Slaves." And in this lay the problem: what rights did the English have as conquerors and what rights did the French Canadians have as the conquered?

Baron Francis Maseres, an English jurist, approached the problem from a slightly different standpoint. To him the problems of the French Canadians were constitutional ones, and the proper solution to them was a Parliamentary measure. Above all others, Maseres appreciated the dilemma of the English in Quebec: how to be conquerors and realize the benefits accruing from a conquest, and, at the same time, respect the rights of a different racial group? In 1766 the conquered French Canadians were British subjects. All British subjects were equal, but some were more equal than others.

Reprinted from D. G. Creighton, *The Empire of the Saint Lawrence,* (Toronto, Macmillan Company of Canada, 1956), pp. 35-49, by permission of the Author and the Macmillan Company of Canada Limited.

The Merchant's Programme:

The New Canadians

. . . The northern commercial system, which depended upon the co-operation of the two races, helped to reconcile the French and British to one another. But it forced the British merchants to do battle with their own kinsmen, both within and without the colony. As we have seen, the merchants had two main objects in America: the defence of the dominion of the St. Lawrence in the continent; and the capture of political power at Quebec. In the period from the conquest until the Quebec Act of 1774, it was chiefly the imperial authorities in England and the governing bureaucracy in Quebec which prevented the realization of these objectives. The imperial planners over in London tried to curb the commercial system of the St. Lawrence in the interests of imperial integration and harmony. The old-fashioned bureaucracy of Quebec attempted to preserve and strengthen the authoritarian, military and feudal elements in the colony of the St. Lawrence, in the alleged interest of the French Canadians.

These two policies, which together denied the past and stunted the future of the northern economy, the merchants set themselves to overthrow. The controversies really began in 1763, for both grew directly or indirectly out of the famous royal proclamation of that year.

The proclamation of 1763 was the imperfect introduction of an imperfect imperial plan, which, like the problem it was designed to solve, was continental in its scope. As everybody knows, the grand scheme was preserved arbitrarily, spasmodically and inefficiently; but it was at bottom an attempt to bring strength, cohesion and order out of the contradictions and chaos of a vast maritime and continental empire, recently swollen by conquest. Each colony, however curious and unusual its character, was to conform at least roughly to an approved and standard pattern; and all colonies, however incompatible their interests and however complicated their extra-imperial relations, were to accommodate themselves to the just demands of their neighbours and the great necessities of the empire as a whole. Of this somewhat belated and clumsy movement for the organization and strengthening of empire, the proclamation of 1763 was the inauspicious prelude. With a few important exceptions, it concerned only the new colonies of Quebec, East and West Florida, and Grenada; but it showed the same virtues and vices as the more comprehensive legislation of the later sixties. It was a plan whose irritation arose not so much from its narrow unfairness as from the very breadth of its complacent and righteous impartiality. It was not that it contradicted justice but that it denied life.

The proclamation of 1763 was the repudiation of Canada's character and history as a distinct American economy, continental, commercial and competitive. For Canada was to be sternly limited in the interests of imperial harmony; and it was to be recreated in the interests of imperial standardization. A great inland commercial empire, its life rigidly simplified and organized to combine with geography for the prosecution of a single staple trade, was to become a normal colony, limited in territory, devoted to agriculture, modestly typical and completely undistinguished. Its boundaries were narrowly contracted by the proclamation. The stunted little colony which the British named Quebec was but a contemptible fragment of what they had conquered as New France. Labrador and the islands of the gulf had already been divided between Newfoundland and Nova Scotia; and the proclamation confirmed the partition. The western hinterland, where lay the colony's one great market, was wrenched away from the province of Quebec to form a western Indian reserve, in which British officials could pursue in uninterrupted seclusion the solution of the Indian problem. Canada was to abandon its pretensions and to learn humility. When Egremont, the secretary of state, argued that the western Indian reserve ought to be placed under the jurisdiction of one of the colonies and that Quebec was logically destined for the task, the board of trade judiciously replied that the annexation of the reserve to Canada was especially objectionable inasmuch as it would give the Canadians an unfair advantage in the fur trade and their governor an overweening importance in the politics of the continent. Somewhat ostentatiously, the British tried to turn the faces of Canadians away from the exciting grandeurs of the St. Lawrence. The new boundary, while it was meaningless from the point of view of geography and commerce which the French had emphasized, possessed a certain justification from the point of view of settlement, which they had neglected. Settlement was no longer to be neglected. "Canada", wrote the board of trade, was a place "where Planting, perpetual Settlement and Cultivation ought to be encouraged . . . ." Governor Murray was instructed to survey the unoccupied parts of his province on the basis of English land tenure and to encourage the advent of aspiring agricultural frontiersmen, in order that Quebec might both relieve congestion on the Atlantic seaboard and develop into healthy normality itself.

All this, however, was not the whole of the proclamation of 1763. The document also contained the famous promise of an assembly and the "Benefit of the Laws of our Realm of England" for all the newly created colonies, including Quebec. English law, in its entirety, was much more than the merchants were to demand for years to come; but the assembly, in their view, was absolutely necessary as the only way in which their political control of the colony could be realized. They both revered and hated the proclamation of 1763. So far as the continent was concerned, it seemed the doom of their commercial ambitions; so far as the province was concerned, it appeared the hope of their political supremacy. And resentment emerged dominant out of the confusion of their emotions as it became increasingly obvious that only the objectionable provisions of the proclamation were to be enforced. The new boundaries were drawn, the Indian reserve set up and a series of obnoxious regulations and restrictions of their trade established. But there was no assembly.

To a very considerable extent, this was the work of the first British governors in Quebec and of the governing clique which surrounded them. James Murray, Guy Carleton and Frederick Haldimand, the three soldiers who in succession ruled the province for a quarter-century after the conquest, belonged, despite certain obvious differences, to a single type and carried out a singularly consistent policy. They were all born into professional and land-owning families and they grew up remote from that new world of commerce and middle-class ideals which arose in England on the ruins of the old monarchy and the old tory party. Murray was of Lowland Scots extraction; Carleton came of an Anglo-Irish family established in County Tyrone; and Haldimand was a French Swiss, born in a little town in the canton of Neuchatel. Their experience, almost purely military in character, was profound but narrow. Murray and Carleton entered the British army at the tender age at which it was customary in the eighteenth century for the aspiring sons of the gentry to begin their military careers; and Haldimand became a member of the national profession of Switzerland and hawked his military talents around Europe for decades with little concern for the colour of the flag so long as the colour of the money was satisfactory. By birth, training and experience, the three men became identified with an eighteenth-century type, from which even their marked personal characteristics could not dissociate them. Murray was impetuous and erratic, with a warm heart and a hot head. Carleton's manner was more formal and his temper more inclined to vindictiveness; and he possessed — what Murray completely lacked — the capacity to work out logical and coherent schemes upon the basis of given premises. Haldimand, who combined a practical instinct with an old-

fashioned courtesy and a love of routine, had neither the emotional directness of Murray nor the calculating intellectuality of Carleton. But these minor variations of tone and emphasis could not alter the rigidly woven pattern of character and mentality which all three men possessed in common. They were members of the English governing class, trained in its most regimented department, the army; and they cherished the convictions characteristic of their profession and their order with bland assurance or with irritable pugnacity.

Their role in Canada, which was essentially counter-revolutionary in spirit, was determined for them; it was dictated by their character, their experience, and by the structure of society and politics on the St. Lawrence. Instinct with the desire for order, obedience and subordination, they looked upon the civilian population as a troop of inexperienced children, either dutiful and well-mannered or disobedient and naughty. They saw themselves, somewhat naïvely, as parents whose indulgence must be corrected by discipline and as magistrates whose severity must be tempered by kindness. They liked Quebec; they began to feel rather agreeably paternal about its people. In Quebec there was much that soothed their professional consequence and satisfied their military and aristocratic convictions. They dwelt fondly upon these features of Canadian life; in their minds and their dispatches they assumed larger proportions than they did in actuality. There was a great military tradition in the colony which Murray relished; "the Canadians", he reported enthusiastically, "are to a man soldiers." The province had a strategic importance which impressed the soldier Carleton. If Quebec were linked with New York by an adequate chain of fortifications, it would help to preserve British power on the continent against the attack of the French or the discontented colonists; and a garrison might be found to defend British interests among the sober and old-fashioned inhabitants of the St. Lawrence. There were, in the society of Quebec, the decayed remnants of a feudal hierarchy, which Carleton sympathetically exaggerated. The old government, it appeared, had taught obedience and subordination; and the Canadian people were obviously simple, docile and politically unambitious. The place had charm. Of all the American colonies, it was the most un-American; astonishingly, in the midst of the American forest, it appeared to preserve the old certainties and the old simplicities. All this was very soothing and highly acceptable to the first British governors. They wished to preserve this static little society; they resented intruders. And they became pro-French and anti-commercial.

They did not, of course, dislike trade in itself; and when trade involved some political consideration such as the protection of Canadian subjects or the extension of Canadian influence and frontiers, both Murray and Carleton were ready to take the side of the merchants. But for the commercial party as a political and social force they had nothing but a gentlemanly aversion and a professional contempt. To Murray, in his outbursts of choleric rage, the merchants were "ignorant, licentious, factious men"; and, in his occasional lapses into patronizing urbanity, they became "poor mercantile devils". Both Murray and Carleton maintained a contemptuous raillery at the expense of the birth and social position of their opponents. Haldimand, who had much of the charm and the inappropriateness of a medieval ruin, was appalled at the pos-

sible social consequences of the jury system in Canada. There were foreign troops serving His Majesty in America; and he shook his head solemnly over the dreadful prospect of a German baron being tried by a jury of Canadian shopkeepers. Carleton, who possibly had less scruple and more political capacity than the other two, organized this odd assortment of military yearnings, aversions and prejudices into a political and social philosophy which became law as the Quebec Act. But Murray, for all his erratic inconsistencies, prepared the way for the revival of the decadent French system, and Haldimand tried to preserve it with an old man's myopic stubbornness.

The governors believed that they fought the battle of justice and humanity for the French Canadians. There can be no question of the sincerity of these convictions; but, at the same time, there can be little doubt that the governors, in yielding to the promptings of their humanitarian instincts, were moved to preserve a political and social system which secured the prolongation of their own power and satisfied the prejudices of their class and profession. The conflict which followed in Quebec was not a conflict between altruism and self-interest, or between right and wrong. It was a struggle between an old force and a new — a struggle for power. On the one hand were the British governors, the Francophil bureaucracy and the French-Canadian landowners, attempting to preserve the paternalistic, military and semi-feudal colony of the St. Lawrence. On the other hand was the middle-class commercial group. In the commercial group was concentrated a great proportion of economic power—the wealth, the energy and ability of the colony. Yet the merchants were jealously shut out from political control.

Here was the origin of their anger and the genesis of political strife. Race, language and religion had, in this period, practically nothing to do with it. It was a re-enactment, upon a distant and insignificant stage, of the classic West-European struggle—the struggle between insurgent commercial capitalism and a decadent and desperately resisting feudal and absolutist state.

The merchants, then, had two policies which in their minds were simply the two aspects, continental and provincial, of a single commercial programme. They desired to recover the economic unity of the St. Lawrence which had been broken by the proclamation of 1763. They hoped to make Canada a truly commercial state by breaking the power of the bureaucracy and gaining the political influence which the proclamation had promised them. They became active first in provincial politics. Their first quarrel was with Governor Murray.

The military régime, which came to an end only in August, 1764, had lasted nearly a year after the proclamation of 1763. For the merchants it had meant billeting, military courts and such irritating absurdities as the garrison order which required everyone abroad after ten o'clock at night to carry a lantern. The régime probably helped to reconcile the French Canadians to the conquest, for the military governors found it easy to employ French-Canadian methods and institutions which were, of course, compatible with absolutist rule for the simple reason that they had developed under it. But the French Canadians, who had endured the whole crisis of the conquest with a resignation which bordered upon apathy, were not the politically active part of the population. The merchants were. To them it

was a grievance that the military régime had lasted so long; it was also a grievance that James Murray lasted on after it. No commission as civil governor could make him anything but a soldier; and as time went on it became obvious that the civil government over which he presided bore an increasingly irritating resemblance to the military régime which it had supposedly replaced. He called no assembly. He could not find it in his heart to deliver the French Canadians into the hands of a few score merchants by establishing an assembly on the basis of the old religious tests; so he delivered the control of the whole colony into his own hands and those of a group of his political appointees. The Francophil bureaucracy, destined to a long and vigorous existence, was established in the council and the courts. The new council proceeded to pass ordinances which the merchants, not without some element of justice, denounced as "Vexatious, Oppressive, unconstitutional". Their bitterness mounted with uninterrupted rapidity; and in the autumn of 1764, since the establishment of civil government, they were not without means of protest and reprisal. They sat on juries and they had been appointed justices of the peace. At Quebec the first grand jury censured the government with solemn self-importance. In Montreal, the new magistrates, headed by the merchant Thomas Walker, began to exalt civilians and humble the military with a natural, if somewhat excessive, zeal. A party of army hoodlums, irritated at this profane perversion of established social values, took the blunt, honest course of soldiers and gentlemen. They invaded Walker's house, fell upon him, beat him thoroughly and amputated a part of his ear.

The merchants now took action. They had a definite objective, the recall of Murray. The methods by which they organized their opposition and the arguments with which they justified it are of some interest, for they were employed again and again in the future. They petitioned the king against the governor. Petitions and memorials long remained the formal device of the commercial lobby at London and Quebec. Like a good many of Murray's and Carleton's dispatches, these petitions were party documents which often degenerated into full-blooded propaganda. They were discussed and debated in taverns and coffee-houses, drafted by small *ad hoc* committees and left for a few days to collect signatures. The collective action of the Canadian merchants, based as it was upon a unity of economic interests and a natural social solidarity, was usually so spontaneous and easy as to make a permanent organization unnecessary. But sometimes, as in the case of the Quebec and Montreal committees which fought against the Quebec Act and corresponded with the American revolutionaries, a small executive body exercised temporary authority.

More important and more difficult was the relationship with London. Of all the social groups in Great Britain, the merchants were the most persistent in support of the policy of conciliation with America during the troubled decade from 1765 to 1775. The Canadian traders, like those of the Atlantic seaboard, found political support in England through their commercial connections; but, so far as numbers went, the British merchants trading to Canada were only a small fraction of the North American group as a whole. The merchants trading to the Atlantic colonies could, on occasion, muster nearly twelve hundred signatures in London alone. But only fifty-six London merchants signed the memorial of April 18,

1765, which dealt with the Walker outrage; and twenty-five individual traders and firms supported the Quebec petition for the dismissal of the governor. The personnel of the group of Canadian merchants altered considerably in this period, for it was not until the formation of the North West Company that a few London firms got control of the greater part of the Canadian trade. The merchants met regularly at the New York Coffee House. The group was small, but it was active and fairly well organized, and as early as 1765 an executive committee had been created. Brook Watson, Robert Hunter, Henry Guinand, Isidore Lynch, Robert Grant and John Strettel were some of the most assiduous in promoting Canadian affairs in the period before the Quebec Act. Every mail which left Canada carried a sheaf of letters for the English merchants, which they not infrequently employed in their representations to the government. Every season at least a few Canadian merchants travelled over to London to discuss business and politics with their correspondents, as Bayne and Mackenzie did in the autumn of 1764. But in the recurrent crises of their affairs, the Canadians often required a special representative in England who would devote himself particularly to uniting the various commercial groups interested in Canada and to concerting Canadian policy. To meet this necessity, there appeared the agent, who in the future was to be sometimes a Canadian and more frequently an Englishman nominated by either the Canadian or British merchants. On this occasion, Bayne and Mackenzie, who were commissioned by the Quebec and Montreal merchants to begin the attack against Murray in England, came to terms with the first Canadian agent in April, 1765. He was Fowler Walker, a lawyer of Lincoln's Inn, and the merchants offered him £200 for one year of his services.

The merchants employed every argument and every insinuation which their baffled fury could suggest. But they were not alone in their prejudices and their vehemence. The first British governors in Canada were not remarkable for their good manners, their good temper, their scrupulosity, or the generosity with which they treated political opponents; and the merchants gave back pretty much what they got. They were not lawyers, but indignant business men, intent upon winning a political victory; and the chief arguments upon which they grounded their case were chosen unconsciously for their direct appeal to the world of eighteenth-century England. England and its empire rested on the twin dogmas of parliamentarism and mercantilism. The Canadian merchants, who felt perfectly at home within this world, had merely to invoke the spirit and quote the texts of imperial philosophies long since grown respectable. When they denounced Murray's ordinances as "Vexatious, Oppressive, unconstitutional", when they demanded the "Blessings of British Liberty" and requested a governor "acquainted with other maxims of Government than Military only", they appealed to that religion of individualism, parliamentarism and *laissez-faire* which had conquered in England in the seventeenth century. "They made speeches", wrote Maseres later, "and wretched ones, about the liberty of the Subject and the prerogative of the crown, the petition of rights, the bill of rights and magna charta. . . ."

In addition, for the benefit of a commercially minded England, they repeated with tiresome iteration all the old commonplaces of seventeenth-century mercantilism. Canada, as they and their London correspondents were at pains to point out, was a valuable colony. It conformed perfectly to the requirements of mercantilism. It supplied the staples, furs, fish and oil; it consumed and did not compete with British manufactures; and it provided an outlet for British shipping. It was unnecessary for them to prove the obvious truth that this trade, which in their view alone made the colony an object worthy of imperial attention, was almost entirely in the hands of British merchants in Canada and England. The Canadians asserted that they would never have engaged in the trade and the British affirmed that they would never have granted the long-term credits necessary for its prosecution, if it had not been for the promise of liberal institutions on the banks of the St. Lawrence. Both Canadians and British joined in insisting that unless Canada's affairs were governed by civilians in the commercial interests, its trade and consequently its prosperity would remain undeveloped.

The campaign against Murray succeeded. The governor was a vulnerable man. His own character and policy, the inefficiency of his servants, the rancours of his military associates and the rowdyism of the army had made the colony a chaos. In the autumn of 1765 Murray was recalled. Subsequently, when the privy council held a formal investigation into the conduct of the governor, the case against him collapsed. The merchants did not press their charges; and, even if they had done so, the probable acquittal of Murray would not have meant very much. Murray, like Strafford, was not a criminal. He was simply a choleric, arrogant, impetuous man who was cordially hated by a politically ambitious minority in much the same way as Strafford was.

The formal investigation, like impeachment, was a clumsy, legal means of exploring the rights of a complicated political struggle. The merchants, having secured Murray's removal, were complacently uninterested in further proceedings. They had wanted the governor's recall, not his head. And since he did not return, they congratulated themselves upon a victory which, as the next few years were to show, was in reality completely delusive.

"Petition of the Quebec Traders"; and "Presentments of the Grand Jury of Quebec", (circa 1764 and 1765), *Documents Relating to the Constitutional History of Canada*, vol. 1, pp. 232-234; 212-216.

The Licentious

Fanaticks

. . . We presume to hope that your Majesty will be pleased to attribute our approaching your Royal Throne with disagreeable Complaints, to the Zeal and Attachment we have to your Majesty's Person and Government, and for the Liberties & Priviledges with which your Majesty has indulged all your Dutifull Subjects.

Our Settlement in this Country with respect to the greatest part of us; take it's date from the Surrender of the Colony to your Majesty's Arms; Since that Time we have much contributed to the advantage of our Mother Country, by causing an additional Increase to her Manufactures, and by a considerable Importation of them, diligently applied ourselves to Investigate and promote the Commercial Interests of this Province and render it flourishing

To Military Government, however oppressive and severely felt, we submitted without murmur, hoping Time with a Civil Establishment would remedy this Evil

With Peace we trusted to enjoy the Blessings of British Liberty, and happily reap the fruits of our Industry: but we should now despair of ever attaining those desirable ends, had we not Your Majesty's experienced Goodness to apply to.

The Ancient Inhabitants of the Country impoverished by the War, had little left wherewith to purchase their common necessaries but a Paper Currency of very doubtfull Value: The Indian War has suspended our Inland Trade for two years past, and both these Causes united have greatly injured our Commerce.

For the redress of which we repose wholly on your Majesty, not doubting but the Wisdom of your Majesty's Councils will in due time put the Paper Currency into a Course of certain and regular Payment, and the Vigour of Your Majesty's Arms terminate that War by a peace advantageous and durable.

We no less rely on your Majesty for the Redress of those Grievances we suffer from the Measures of Government practised in this your Majesty's Province, which are

The Deprivation of the open Trade declared by your Majesty's most gracious Proclamation, by the Appropriation of some of the most commodious Posts of the Resort of the Savages, under the Pretext of their being your Majesty's private Domain.

The Enacting Ordinances Vexatious, Oppressive, unconstitutional, injurious to civil Liberty and the Protestant Cause.

Suppressing dutifull and becoming Remonstrances of your Majesty's Subjects against these Ordinances in Silence and Contempt.

The Governor instead of acting agreeable to that confidence reposed in him by your Majesty, in giving a favorable Reception to those of your Majesty's Subjects, who petition and apply to him on such important Occasions as require it, doth frequently treat them with a Rage and Rudeness of Language and Demeanour, as dishonorable to the Trust he holds of your Majesty as painful to those who suffer from it.

His further adding to this by most flagrant Partialities, by formenting Parties and taking measures to keep your Majesty's old and new Subjects divided from one another, by encouraging the latter to apply for Judges of their own National Language.

His endeavouring to quash the Indictment against Claude Panet (his Agent in this Attempt who laboured to inflame the Minds of the People against your Majesty's British Subjects) found by a very Worthy Grand Inquest, and causing their other judicious and honest Presentments to be answered from the Bench with a Contemptuous Ridicule.

This discountenancing the Protestant Religion by almost a Total Neglect of Attendance upon the Service of the Church, leaving the Protestants to this Day destitute of a place of Worship appropriated to themselves.

The Burthen of these Grievances from Government is so much the more severely felt, because of the natural Poverty of the Country; the Products of it been extremely unequal to support its Consumption of Imports.

Hence our Trade is miserably confined and distressed, so that we lye under the utmost Necessity of the Aids and Succours of Government, as well from Our Mother Country as that of the Province, in the Place of having to contend against Oppression and Restraint.

We could enumerate many more Sufferings which render the Lives of your Majesty's Subjects, especially your

Majesty's loyal British Subjects, in the Province so very unhappy that we must be under the Necessity of removing from it, unless timely prevented by a Removal of the present Governor.

Your Petitioners therefore most humbly pray your Majesty to take the Premises into your gracious Consideration, and to appoint a Governor over us, acquainted with other maxims of Government than Military only; And for the better Security of your Majesty's dutiful and loyal Subjects, in the Possession and Continuance of their Rights and Liberties, we beg leave also most humbly to petition that it may please your Majesty, to order a House of Representatives to be chosen in this as in other of your Majesty's Provinces; there being a number more than Sufficient of Loyal and well affected Protestants, exclusive of military Officers, to form a competent and respectable House of Assembly; and your Majesty's new Subjects, if your Majesty shall think fit, may be allowed to elect Protestants without burdening them with such Oaths as in their present mode of thinking they cannot conscientiously take.

PRESENTMENTS OF THE GRAND JURY
OF QUEBEC

. . . 1. That the Great Number of inferior Courts establish'd in this province with an intention to administer Justice are tiresome litigious and expensive to this poor Colony as they very often must be attended with the disagreeable necessity of appeals and of course of many exorbitant fees.

2^d The Great number appointed Justices of the Peace out of so few men of Character legally qualified, and fit to be trusted with determining the liberty and property of his Majesty's Subjects to serve their Country as Jurors, is Burthensome and not practised in other Infant Colonys like this. It can answer no good end, to waste mens time, in attending on Courts where no man is upon the Bench qualified to explain the Law, and sum up the Evidences to the Jury, to prevent its being misled by the Barristers.

4. That in the Southern Colonies, where men qualified to serve the publick are scarce, there are no Jurys calld but when the Chief Justice of the province presides, therefore neither the Lives nor Libertys of his Majesty's Subjects, nor any property above the value of 3 £ Sterl^g are left finally to the decision of the Justices of the Peace, and for the easy and speedy dispatch of Justice there are Annually held three Courts of Common pleas and Two of Sessions or assizes, where Jurys are summon'd in Rotation from the different parts of the province and return'd by Ballots, Yet we are of opinion from the present state of this Colony it would be reasonable to Authorize any three of his Majesty's Justices of the Peace finally to determine the fate of any sum not exceeding Ten pounds without Jury or appeal.

5. We represent also as a very great grievance that the market places are converted into Hutts, Stalls, &c. for Nurserys of Idlers, who would out of Necessity be employ'd in several Branches of Industry, such as Fishing, Farming &c^a if not permitted contrary to good policy to occupy and infest the publick Ground.

7. We recommend the exertion of the Laws of the Mother Country for the due observance of the Sabbath that the same may not longer be profaned, by selling, buying, keeping open shops, Balls, Routs, Gaming or any other Idle Divertions, for the better accomplishing of which, a Learned Clergyman of a moral and exemplary Life, qualified to preach the Gospel in its primative purity in both languages would be absolutely necessary.

9. We represent that as the Grand Jury must be consider'd at present as the only Body representative of the Colony, they, as British Subjects, have a right to be consulted, before any Ordinance that may affect the Body that they represent, be pass'd into a Law, And as it must happen that Taxes be levy'd for the necessary Expences or Improvement of the Colony in Order to prevent all abuses & embezlements or wrong application of the publick money.

10. We propose that the publick Accounts, be laid before the Grand Jury, at least twice a year to be examined and Check'd by them and that they may be regularly settled every Six months before them, which practice strictly adhered to, will very much prevent the abuses and confusion, too common in these matters.

12. The Ordinance made by the Governor and Council for establishing Courts of Judicature in this province is grievous and some Clauses of it, We apprehend to be unconstitutional, therefore it ought forthwith to be amended to prevent his Majesty's Subjects being aggrieved any longer thereby.

13. proper regulations regarding the measurement & quality of Fire wood are wanted as well as the following articles. Viz^t

For regulating Carts and Carriages of every kind.

For clearing and keeping clean the public streets Docks and Landing places.

For sweeping Chimnies to prevent accidents by Fire.

For establishing a publick protestant school and a Poor house.

14. For suppressing gaming houses, in particular that of the Quebec Arms kept by John King in the lower Town, which we have been informed has been very particularly countenanced; and which we ourselves present, from our own Knowledge as a notorious nusance, and prejudicial to the Industry and Trade of this City. . . .

As the presentment made by the protestant members of the Jury, wherein the impannelling of Roman Catholicks upon Grand petty Juries, even where two protestants are the parties, is complained of. As this very presentment has been openly & ungenerously used as a handle to set his Majesty's old & new Subjects at varience in this province, we cannot help endeavor^g to set the public right in this particular in which they have been so grossly imposed on: What gave birth to this presentmt. was the following short, but pithy Paragraph, in the Ordinance of the 17th Day of Septr last.

"In all Tryalls in this Court all his Majesty's Subjects in this Colony to be admitted on Juries without any distinction:" This is qualifying the whole province at once for an Office which the best & most sensible people in it are hardly able to discharge: It then occur'd to the Jury that was laying a Subject's life, liberty & property too open, & that both old & new Subjects might be apprehensive of the consequence from the unlimited admission of Jurymen His Majesty's lately acquired Subjects cannot take it amiss, that his ancient subjects remonstrate ag^t this practice as being contrary to the laws of the realm of England, the benefit of which they think they have a right to, nor ought it to give offence when they demand that a protestant Jury should be impannelled when the litigating parties are protestants such were the real motives of the Presentment, and we can aver that nothing further was meant by the quotation from the Statute.

That the subscribers of the presentment meant to remove every Roman Catholick from holding any office or filling any public employment is to all intents and purposes a most vile groundless insinuation & utterly inconsistent: Sentiments & intentions such as these we abhor, & are only sorry that principles do not allow us to admit Roman Catholicks as Jurors upon a cause betwixt two protestants; perhaps theirs hold us in the same light in a Case betwixt two Catholicks, and we are very far from finding fault with them, the same liberty that we take of thinking for ourselves we must freely indulge to others. . . .

"Statement by French Jurors in Reference to the Foregoing Presentments, 1764." *Documents Relating to the Constitutional History of Canada*, vol. 1, pp. 216–223.

Justice vs.

Tyranny

Charrest, Amiot, Tachet, Boisseaux, Poney, Dumont & Perrault new Subjects, Grand Jurors in the districts of Quebec, having demanded from His Excellency in Council the Translation into French of two Presentments written in English in the House of the Three Canons, all the Jurors being assembled, one of which presentments of the 16th of the present month of October, was signed by the petitioners along with the other jurors, and the other was signed by the jurors who were ancient subjects understanding English alone, and having obtained the same, they consider themselves bound to declare the part which they had taken in the articles which compose the first Presentment.

They begin by saying that before the Signature of this Presentment, there had been many sessions, where the question had been discussed by making Several Drafts of Presentment on loose sheets, and of these the petitioners had knowledge of only a part while many of those, with the contents of which they were acquainted, had been modified or rejected by the Petitioners; that a Summary certainly had been made of all the papers, and that after it was made, it was offered to us for Signature, without being interpreted, but was read in English only, that when it was requested by some of us, that it should be read to us, the answer was that this summary was only a Résumé of the Drafts of the Articles which had been proposed and accepted during the late Sessions, that time pressed for their presentation and that it was very unnecessary.

They intend therefore to set forth the part which they have had in the different Articles which compose this Presentment.

1. Article. Not only had we no knowledge of this Article, but we should certainly have opposed this proposition with all our might, as being contrary to the interests of His Majesty's New Subjects in the Colony, and as being opposed to the wise ordinance of the Governor and Council, who, seeing the necessity of establishing a Court of Justice where the New Subjects should be able to find a Sanctuary in which they might be judged as Frenchmen by Frenchmen, according to Ancient Customs, and in their own Tongue, has since been requested in a Petition to name the Judge of this Jurisdiction and which the Petitioners themselves have signed as Citizens; for besides the convenience that it would be to them to be judged in this Jurisdiction, they would save more than half the costs.

2, 3, 4, Art.** We did not understand these Articles if they were interpreted to us, and as we are ignorant of what is going on in the different Colonies, we have no interest in proposing any particular alterations in these Articles.

5. We understand that wooden Houses and Stalls in the Market are contrary to good Policy, and are sometimes the Causes of Fires. . . .

7. We have heard this Article in part, and only in connection with Sunday observance. But the Proposal of having a Minister to preach the Gospel in both languages has certainly not been explained to us. . . .

9 & 10. These two Articles have not been explained to us, and we are not sufficiently far-seeing to pay attention to Measures which at present appear to us very remote, owing to the hope which we entertain that no question of Taxation for this Colony will arise. . . .

12. This Article has never been communicated to us, and we imagine it was only proposed, because it is stated in that ordinance, that Canadian Lawyers, New Subjects of H. M. might practise. The ordinance appears to us the more equitable, in that it is only right that the new Canadian Subjects should employ Persons whom they understand, and by whom They are understood, all the more because there is not one English Lawyer who knows the French Language, and with whom it would not be necessary to employ an Interpreter who would scarcely ever give the exact meaning of the Matter in hand. And further, without this wise regulation which ensures the Tranquillity of domestic affairs would not the opposing Parties find themselves involved in exorbitant expense?

13. We are thoroughly familiar with the Items which form a Part of this Article, such as the Proposal to establish Regulations for the Measuring of Wood, for Carters and Vehicles of every description, for the best method of keeping the Streets, public Squares, and Docks clean, and for the Sweeping of Chimneys to prevent Accidents by fire. We have given our consent solely to these Items, and our

present situation does not allow us to extend our care in other directions.

14. There has been no question of discussing Gaming Houses except in desultory conversation, and we did not suppose it had been spoken of seriously enough to make it worth while to consider, if it was proposed to denounce them as suspicious Houses, especially that of the said King, to whom none of us can attribute as a crime the Protection which is granted him by those whom he has the Faculty of Serving so well. Besides this we did happen to say in conversation that if they were playing at unseasonable Hours, and at Games proscribed by the Police, then this Article might represent it as dangerous to youth and to Trade, but we have absolutely no knowledge that this Article was in the Presentment which we have signed. . . .

We quite realize that in order to avoid Confusion in the future, Canadian Jurors should give their Opinions only after the Subjects on which it is asked have been translated into the French Language.

In view of the knowledge that we, the G^d Jurors, Canadian new Subjects of H. M. have,—having read it in the French tongue,—of the Presentment which our confreres, the Ancient Subjects, Grand Jurors, have made at the Court of Session, and of the two Subscriptions, with the intention of excluding us from the privilege of serving ourselves and Our associates, our Country and our King, pretending that they conscientiously believe us to be incapable of holding any office or even of repulsing and fighting the Enemies of H. M.^{ty} We make the following statement.

That H. M.^{ty} being informed that all the Subjects forming this Province were

Catholics still believed them capable as such of taking the Oath of Loyalty, and therefore fit to be admitted to the service of their Country, in such a way as they shall be thought qualified for. It would be shameful to believe that the Canadians, New Subjects, cannot serve their King either as Serjeant, or Officers, it would be a most humiliating thought, and very discouraging to free Subjects who have been admitted to the Privileges of the Nation, and their Rights, as explained by H. M. For more than six Months we have had Catholic Canadian Officers in the Upper Country, and a Number of Volunteers aiding to repulse the Enemies of the Nation; and cannot a man who exposes himself freely to shed his blood in the Service of his King and of the Nation be admitted to positions where he can serve the Nation and the Public as a Juror, since he is a subject? The 3rd of James I. Chap. 5, Sec. 8, only refers to Catholics who may enter the Kingdom, and as there has never been any law in any Kingdom without some exception was a proof that in time England would admit to the National rights so numerous a Colony of Catholics, or if this had been foreseen, that the Law would seek to make them slaves. We think differently from our confreres, and even if we were of their opinion, we should have enough Confidence in the King's Goodness to believe that he would grant all the Numerous people of this Colony sufficient respite to depart, though at the sacrifice of all their possessions, and in desperation cultivate the Ground, in some place, where being considered as Subjects, they and their Children might lead their Lives sheltered from Injustice. This they could never do here were they deprived of all Offices, or positions as Jurors.

The Leniency of the existing Government has made us forget our losses, and has attached us to H. M. and to the Government; our fellow citizens make us feel our Condition to be that of Slaves. Can the faithful and loyal Subjects of the King be reduced to this?

This ends the Protest that we make against the use of our Signatures on the Presentment of the Sixteenth instant, in every point in which they might be prejudicial to us. Done at Quebec the 26th October, 1764.

PERRAULT,   BONNEAU,

TACHET,   CHAREST,

AMIOT,   PENEY,

DAMONT.

Baron Francis Maseres, "Considerations on the Expediency of Procuring an Act of Parliament for the Settlement of the Province of Quebec, 1766", *Documents Relating to the Constitutional History of Canada*, vol. 1, pp. 257-269.

Expediency versus

Tyranny

The Difficulties that have arisen in the government of the province of Quebec, and which are likely still to occur in it, notwithstanding the best intentions of those who are intrusted by His Majesty with the administration of affairs there, are so many and so great that the Officers, whom His Majesty has been pleased of late to nominate to the principal departments in that government, cannot look upon them without the greatest uneasiness and apprehension, and despair of being able to overcome them without the assistance of an act of Parliament to ground and justify their proceedings. Two nations are to be kept in peace and harmony, and moulded, as it were, into one, that are at present of opposite religions, ignorant of each others language, and inclined in their affections to different systems of laws. The bulk of the inhabitants are hitherto either French from old France, or native Canadians, that speak only the French language, being, as it is thought, about ninety thousand souls,

or as the French represent it in their Memorial, ten thousand heads of families. The rest of the inhabitants are natives of Great Britain or Ireland, or of the British dominions in North-America, and are at present only about six hundred souls; but, if the province is governed in such a manner as to give satisfaction to the inhabitants, will probably every day increase in number by the accession of new settlers for the sake of trade and planting, so that in time they may equal or exceed the number of the French. The French are almost uniformly Roman Catholics: there were only three protestant families among them at the time of the conquest of the province; and probably that number is not much increased among them, as no endeavours have been used for their conversion. But, what is more to be lamented, is that they are violently bigotted to the Popish religion, and look upon all Protestants with an eye of detestation. This unhappy circumstance has been, and is still likely to be, a ground of enmity and disunion between the old and new inhabitants. The French insist, not only upon a toleration of the public worship, but on a share in the administration of Justice, as jury-men and justices of the peace, and the like, and on a right, in common with the English, of being appointed to all the offices of the government. The English, on the contrary, affirm, that the laws of England made against the Papists ought to be in force there, and consequently that the native Canadians, unless they think proper to turn Protestants, ought to be excluded from all those offices and various branches of power, and in some degree they seem to be supported in this opinion by a part of the governor's commission; I mean that part which enables him to call and constitute a general assembly of the free-holders and planters of the province: for it is there expressly provided, that no person elected to serve in such an assembly, shall sit and vote there till he has subscribed the declaration against Popery prescribed by the statute 25. Car. 2 which would effectually exclude all the Canadians.

The grounds upon which the French demand a toleration of the Catholic religion, are partly the reasonableness of the thing itself, they being almost universally of that religion, and partly the stipulation made on that behalf in the fourth article of the definitive treaty of peace, and which is expressed in these words: "His Britannic Majesty on his side agrees "to grant the liberty of the Catholic re- "ligion to the inhabitants of Canada; he "will consequently give the most effectual "orders that his new Roman Catholic sub- "jects may profess the worship of their "religion, according to the rites of the "Romish church, as far as the laws of "Great Britain permit."

These last words, "as far as the laws of Great Britain permit," render the whole stipulation in favour of this toleration very doubtful; for it may reasonably be contended, that the laws of England do not at all permit the exercise of the Catholic religion. . . .

But this act goes a great deal further; for it requires all ecclesiastical persons whatsoever, and likewise all lay-persons holding temporal offices, or employed in the service of the Crown, and likewise all persons holding lands of the Crown, and doing homage for them, to take the oath of supremacy to the Queen, or her successors, under pain of losing their benefices, or temporal offices, &c and this not only in the realm of England, but in any of the Queen's highness's dominions. So that by this part of the act, all the Canadian clergy, and a great part of the laity,

might be required to take the oath of supremacy, which it is well known the most moderate Catholics cannot take, it being contrary to the fundamental article of their religion; for the difference between the moderate Catholics and the more furious and zealous Papists, who are mostly guided by the Jesuits, consists principally in this circumstance, that the latter ascribe to the Pope an unlimited power in temporal as well as spiritual matters, and affirm that he may depose kings, and absolve subjects from their allegiance, and do other the like extravagant mischiefs; whereas the former deny his temporal, and acknowledge only his spiritual supremacy. . . .

Upon these reasons we may conclude, that the exercise of the Catholic religion cannot, consistently with the laws of Great Britain, be tolerated in the province of Quebec.

Yet that it should be tolerated is surely very reasonable, and to be wished by all lovers of peace and justice and liberty of conscience.

By what authority then shall it be tolerated? this is the only question that remains. Shall the King alone undertake to tolerate it? will it be advisable that he should exercise, though for so good an end, a power of dispensing with the laws? will it not give room to a thousand censures and odious reflections and comparisons? The authority of Parliament seems to be a much safer foundation to establish this measure upon, in a manner which neither the new English inhabitants of the province can Contest, nor the French Catholics suspect to be inadequate.

The next great difficulty that occurs, is the settlement of the laws, by which the province of Quebec is for the future to be governed. The law upon this subject seems to be this; 1st, That the laws of the conquered continue in force till the will of the conqueror is declared to the contrary; this follows from the necessity of the case, since otherwise the conquered provinces would be governed by no laws at all. 2dly, That after the declaration of the will of the conqueror, the conquered are to be governed by such laws as the conqueror shall think fit to impose, whether those are the old laws by which they have been governed before, or the laws by which the conquerors are governed themselves, or partly one, and partly the other, or a new set of laws different from both. 3dly, That by the conqueror is to be understood the conquering nation, that is, in the present case, the British nation; that consequently by the will of the conqueror is to be understood the will of the British nation, which in all matters relating to legislation is Expressed by the King and Parliament, as in all matters relating to the executive power it is expressed by the King alone; that therefore the Parliament only have a power to make laws for the province of Quebec, or to introduce any part of the laws of Great Britain there, or to delegate such a power of making or introducing laws to any other hands, notwithstanding it may happen that in fact such a power may inadvertently have been delegated to the governor and council of the province by a private instruction of the King alone. For if the contrary doctrine were true, that the King alone had the whole legislative power in the province of Quebec, it would follow, that not only all the conquered Canadians, but all the new English settlers there, would become slaves or subjects to an absolute and arbitrary government, the moment they set their foot there. The King might introduce the severest laws, and most cruel punishments, the inquisition, the rack, and the wheel, and might make all his subjects there, both old and new, tenants at will of their lands and other property, and tax them in any degree whensoever he thought fit. He might keep a standing army there, without consent of Parliament, and raise money to pay them by his own authority, and with such an army, a prince of James II's. disposition, might oppress the liberties of the other adjoining colonies, or even of Great Britain itself. These are dreadful consequences, but follow clearly from such a doctrine; for which reason the doctrine itself ought not to be maintained. The other opinion, that the conquered people, when once ceded to the Crown of Great Britain, are thereby admitted to be British Subjects, and immediately intitled to participate of the liberties of other British Subjects, and are therefore to be governed according to the rules of the limited monarchy of Great Britain, by which the executive power is vested solely in the King, but the power of making laws and raising taxes in the King and Parliament, is a much safer and more reasonable opinion. . . .

If the Parliament should think proper itself to lay a tax upon the Province, information has been received from persons well acquainted with the state and trade of the province, that British spirits would be the commodity that could best bear a duty, and would produce the best revenue; that there are annually imported into the province about 250,000 gallons of these spirits, and that they might bear duty of three-pence a gallon, without hurting the trade, but not more; and this would produce about 3,000l. a year.

The malicious and desperate enemies of an upright and popular Administration, may perhaps traduce such a measure as inconsistent with their late indulgent conduct with respect to the other American colonies in the late repeal of the stamp-act. But the difference of the cases is too striking to make such a calumny in the least degree formidable. The other American colonies have internal legislatures of their own, who have been permitted, ever since their first establishment, to be the assessors of all their internal taxes; and, as they had not abused this privilege with which they had been so long indulged, and further, as their exercising this privilege seemed to be no way prejudicial to the mother-country, it seemed to have been a harsh and ungracious measure in the Parliament, by the advice of the late ministry, to revive and exert a dormant and inherent right of taxing them; which however the whole Parliament, excepting a very few members of both houses, have highly declared themselves to be possessed of. But the Canadians have no such internal legislature, no such usage of taxing themselves by representatives of their own chusing. Unless therefore they have the singular privilege of not being liable to be taxed at all, they must be liable to be taxed either by the King alone, or by the King and Parliament; and the milder of these two opinions is that they are taxable by the King and Parliament. Those therefore who should promote the taxing them by authority of Parliament, would act like the truest friends to civil liberty, and with the same spirit of mildness and moderation that conducted them in the repeal of the stamp-act.

If it should be said, that the province of Quebec ought to have an assembly in the same manner as the other American colonies, and that the taxes ought to be imposed by the consent of such an assembly, it will be sufficient for the present purpose, and to support the measure here suggested of taxing them by authority of Parliament, to answer that as yet no such assembly has been constituted; and till an assembly is erected, whether that time be short or long, the safest and mildest method of imposing taxes is to do it by authority of Parliament.

As to the erecting an assembly in that province, it is a measure which probably will not for some years to come be found expedient. If an assembly were now to be constituted, and the directions in the governor's commission, above alluded to, were to be observed, by which none of the members elected there are to be permitted to sit and vote in the assembly till they have subscribed the declaration against Popery, it would amount to an exclusion of all the Canadians, that is, of the bulk of the settled inhabitants of the province— An assembly so constituted, might pretend to be a representative of the people there, but in truth it would be a representative of only the 600 new English settlers, and an instrument in their hands of domineering over the 90,000 French. Can such an assembly be thought just or expedient, or likely to produce harmony and friendship between the two nations? Surely it must have a contrary effect.

On the other hand, it might be dangerous in these early days of their submission, to admit the Canadians themselves to so great a degree of power. Bigotted, as they are, to the Popish religion, unacquainted with, and hitherto prejudiced against the laws and customs of England, they would be very unlikely for some years to come, to promote such measures, as should gradually introduce the Protestant religion, the use of the English language, of the spirit of the British laws. It is more probable they would check all such endeavours, and quarrel with the governor and council, or with the English members of the assembly, for promoting them. Add to this, that they are almost universally ignorant of the English language, so as to be absolutely incapable of debating in it, and consequently must, if such an assembly were erected, carry on the business of it in the French language, which would tend to perpetuate that language, and with it their prejudices and affections to their former masters, and postpone to a very distant time, perhaps forever, that coalition of the two nations, or the melting down the French nation into the English in point of language, affections, religion, and laws, which is so much to be wished for, and which otherwise a generation or two may perhaps effect, if proper measures are taken for that purpose. And further it may be observed, that the Canadians themselves do not desire an assembly, but are contented to be protected in the enjoyment of their religion, liberties, and properties, under the administration of his Majesty's governor and council. If, to give a proper stability to this mode of government, it is carried on by authority of Parliament, and is properly superintended, as no doubt it will be, by the wisdom of his Majesty's Privy-Council, they will think themselves extremely happy under it. The persons who most desire the immediate constitution of an assembly, are some of the six hundred English adventurers, who probably are ambitious of displaying their parts and eloquence in the characters of leading Assemblymen.

But if an assembly is to be constituted, even this too had better be done by act of Parliament than by the King's single authority, as it is no less than severing from the general body of his Majesty's dominions a particular part of them, with respect to the purposes of making laws and imposing taxes. Could the King, if he thought proper, and a particular county of England was to desire it of him, sever that county from the rest of England, and no longer summon any of its members to Parliament, but instead thereof constitute a little Parliament in that County itself, that should make laws and lay taxes for the inhabitants of that single county? It is presumed that he could not: and the erecting an assembly in a conquered province is an act of much the same nature. It is true indeed, that some of the American charters and assemblies owe their rise to this authority: but this was in the reign of the Stuarts, who were fond of extending their prerogative; and, on account of the inconsiderableness of the colonies at that time, these things were then unnoticed; so that they do not prove the strict legality of the practice. Since that time these charters have been put in practice by the colonies, and acquiesced in by the mother-country, and in some measure recognized in Parliament and this usage, acquiescence and recognition, are in truth their best support.

But if an assembly is to be constituted, in which the Catholics or Canadians are to be admitted (as in justice and reason they ought to be, if any assembly at all is to be erected) the authority of Parliament seems to be still more necessary to give validity to such a measure.

For the reasons that have been just now mentioned, it seems evident, that the measure of erecting an assembly in the province of Quebec is somewhat premature. How soon it will become expedient and proper, experience only can shew. But in the mean time, however short that time may be, it seems necessary to have recourse to the authority of Parliament for settling the government of the province, and removing the difficulties that obstruct the settlement in the three great articles

of Religion, Law, and Revenue. It is therefore the humble request of all the gentlemen who have lately been appointed to
the principal offices in the government of
Quebec, to his Majesty's Ministers of
State, that they would use their influence
and endeavours to procure such an act of
Parliament as they shall upon the whole
matter think to be necessary, to remove
the difficulties that have been stated, and
to enable the said gentlemen to administer
the government of that province in their
several departments, with security to
themselves, and advantage to the province.

Part V

Briand,
the New Bishop:
Servant or Servile?

All the social institutions of New France were affected by the Conquest. One, however, was to be less disturbed than others—the Church. The political and economic elite, one group really, fled or left the country, or were displaced by British administrators and merchants. The political and financial centre of the colony was now in England instead of France. The Roman Catholic Church, although subjected to the same pressures as other institutions, was able, by accident and policy, to survive, provide a continuity in a period of transition, and even increase its importance in the newly-conquered society.

In 1760, Monseigneur de Pontbriand, the Bishop of New France, died. The conquered colonists, under the terms of the Capitulation of Montreal, were allowed to practise their faith, with some slight restrictions. The Royal Proclamation of 1763 tolerated the Roman Catholic Church in so far as the laws of Great Britain permitted, that is, it made second class citizens of Roman Catholics. But the Canadian Roman Catholic Church had no bishop. This meant that no new priests could be consecrated, and the British authorities refused to allow French Catholic clergymen to come to Quebec. These conditions, as Francis Maseres was to write, were not to be "wished by all lovers of peace and justice and liberty of conscience."

On the other hand, the British government and its administrators in the colony of Quebec faced a very real dilemma. The enemy of their state was France; France was a Roman Catholic power and the King of France was the eldest son of the Church. It is true that British traditions included liberty of conscience, but the traditions also included a virulent anti-Papism. In typical British fashion, pragmatically, the imperial government and Murray "burned the candle at both ends." Theoretically, the requirements of the laws of Great Britain were met in the constitution, the Proclamation, but in fact, the restrictions against Catholics were set aside in Quebec. Legally, as Maseres pointed out, this could not endure, and the problem was resolved by the Quebec Act of 1774.

The selections which follow all agree on one essential point: a bishop had to be provided. Hilda Neatby's essay on Briand, who was Murray's choice as crypto-bishop, skirts controversy. It emphasizes the internal problems of the Church. The effects of Briand's collaboration are directly dealt with by Marcel Trudel. Neatby's "Minor Canadian" implemented major policies which were to have a profound effect on the future of French Canadian society. One of the most noteworthy effects was what Trudel calls the *Canadianization* of the Roman Catholic Church in Quebec and its

corollary, the abandonment of Gallicanism. Elizabeth Arthur is concerned with why Murray supported the pretensions of the Roman Catholic Church. Political expediency, not altruism, was responsible, for both British policy and that of the Church were served by the collaboration.

Whether the alliance between the British conqueror and the Roman Catholic Church of Quebec was good or bad cannot be answered categorically. The effects of the alliance, however, should be inquired into. One significant result of the collaboration was to link French Canadian survival and French Canadian nationalism with the Church. Another matter of some importance concerns the rôle of the Church, and in particular its spiritual rôle: are secular and spiritual matters compatible? Further, did the Roman Catholic Church in Quebec have any alternative?

Hilda Neatby, "Jean-Olivier Briand:
A 'Minor Canadian'," *Canadian Historical
Association Report*, 1963, pp. 1-16. Re-
printed by permission of the Canadian
Historical Association and the Author.

Servant

Briand illustrates the plight of so
many of our national figures. Caught in
difficult times, hurled into controversies
which in our ardour we cannot let die,
they are bottled and labelled according
to their party, their "significance", their
"contribution", and it is most difficult to
get at the live person, to tear off his label,
and to see him as a man. Briand has
been all but canonized by the Abbé
Gosselin (bottled one might say in the
sweetest and heaviest of syrup); he has
been labelled with benign but passing approval by Professor Burt. He has been,
more recently, somewhat severely treated

by that meticulous scholar Professor
Marcel Trudel . . .

. . . The death of Mgr. Pontbriand
on May 8, 1760 left the see vacant at the
very moment when the Capitulation of
Montreal ceded the country to the English. Briand was not "capitulary vicar",
but, as vicar-general at Quebec and apparently in some fashion designated by
Mgr. Pontbriand for this role, he did
assume some leadership in the crisis. As
is well known, the Quebec Chapter,
anxious to secure a bishop, "elected"
Montgolfier, the able and distinguished
head of the wealthy Seminary of Sulpicians at Montreal. The election was not
approved at Rome; Montgolfier was not
approved by the English authorities at
Quebec. By subterranean and tortuous
methods Briand, the choice of General
Murray, passed from Quebec to London
and from London to Paris (tactfully
avoiding any obvious contact with Rome)
and then, in 1766 back to Quebec, now
officially recognized in London as "the
Superintendent of the Romish Religion".
So he remained until 1784, when his Britannic Majesty was graciously pleased to
consent to his retirement, with a comment on his long and faithful services
and his virtuous life. This was London.
But he had been consecrated bishop in
France on the authority of Rome, and
before long in Quebec he was "the
Bishop" to everyone from the English
governor down. . . .

The Church in Canada had hitherto
been supported and sustained by the
authority of government, the habits of
society, and the simple fact that there
was no other church. Priests and people
could be subjected to a discipline which

might generally be easy because it would always be firm. But now not only were Protestants pouring in, but the old single undivided allegiance to church and king together was torn apart. Men must obey (and the church must teach them to obey) an alien and heretic government. Some would resent this and revile the church that imposed on them such a rule. Others would appeal to their new governors against the authority of the church and so make a mockery of discipline and good order. An adequate, united and dedicated priesthood might hope to hold together the church. But the priesthood in Canada was not entirely united or completely dedicated. This was, after all, the eighteenth century, in England and France alike a strange combination of great piety and much ecclesiastical worldliness. . . .

He exhorted to virtue. Some needed to be reminded so often and so forcibly that a reading of the letters can give a false impression. As M. Trudel has noted *"le bien ne fait pas de bruit"*, and no doubt the great majority of the priests were, in intention at least, men of integrity, diligence, and devotion. But their task was hard, they were isolated, and no doubt often perplexed and tempted. There is no reason to suppose that Briand looked for trouble, but he remarked himself in the early days when he was still only vicar-general "there is hardly any priest that I have not been obliged to rebuke if you except eight or ten. . . . "

It was not only virtue but prudence that the priests needed, and Briand cultivated as he could the wisdom of the serpent. Priests must, of course, work hard at their business, not lose a moment that can be given to study, and they must be constantly aware of their difficult position in relation to the government, alien in religion, to which they owe allegiance. They must carefully observe the law for *"c'est un grand nom chez les Anglais"*, but they must avoid litigation. They must not carry their own suggestions or complaints to the governor, but they are to remember to pay courtesy calls when they are in Quebec as this is expected (at least by Murray). They are not to express views publicly on public affairs, and advice even in confession must be given with much caution. This last exhortation was accompanied with the remark that in the particular instance under discussion the priest would have been reproved for such meddling even under the French régime. . . .

It was all very well to write and exhort. The peculiar difficulty of Briand's position lay in the fact that, accustomed to the order and discipline of the hierarchy supported by ecclesiastical monopoly and the countenance of the state, he now found himself at the head of a "voluntary" and yet a still rigidly authoritarian church, in the unhappy position of complete responsibility and no power. No power, that is, beyond his moral power to appeal to custom and tradition, to piety and to faith, and, incidentally, to the fear of hell, an appeal which he used with a certain freedom. Had Briand been a Protestant he would assuredly have been, as one would say, well to the left, perhaps an old-fashioned Methodist. . . .

One special problem that met Briand shortly after his return as Bishop was the dissolution of the Jesuit order by the Pope. Already Jesuits were forbidden to recruit by the English, but Briand needed the services of those who were left. His views, as it happened, were particularly furthered in this matter by Cramahé, who was most anxious at this critical time to do nothing to weaken ecclesiastical authority. Lieutenant-governor and Bishop worked out a *modus vivendi*. Briand did not publish the bull of dissolution, but he did convey it privately to the Jesuits, who submitted with much humility. Briand himself became the "superior" of a community which was no longer Jesuit, but the Fathers continued to wear their usual garb and to discharge their priestly functions. In fact Briand ordained two brothers to be priests. The Jesuits continued to manage their own property until the death of the last of their order in Canada who had retained complete control of the income from which he gave large sums in charity. No one beyond the Jesuits themselves, the bishop, the governor and his secretary, knew that as an order they had ceased to exist in Canada, a situation without parallel, I believe, except in Russia where Catherine refused publication of the bull. Catherine felt no particular responsibility to Rome, but Briand did, and, having read his rather complacent account of the good arrangements he had made, one wonders how he explained his disobedience to his ecclesiastical superiors. . . .

A most serious responsibility of Briand as vicar-general and as bishop was the well-being and good conduct of the various communities of nuns whose kindly and essential services in caring for the sick as well as in the education of young girls had been warmly praised by their good friend and protector, the fierce Protestant, Murray.

Murray's praises were warmly echoed by a later bishop (Hubert), but an examination of Briand's letters shows that the nuns like the priests occasionally caused anxiety, and even aroused his generally fleeting wrath. This was the eighteenth century and there is evidence that the relaxed outlook of many communities in France might have had some influence even on the more puritanical colony of the St. Lawrence. A long letter to the nuns at the General Hospital who wish to receive novices, relates the many faults, the excessive worldliness, the indiscipline which make them in the eyes of the Bishop very unfit to do so. And the Ursulines are gently admonished for using coloured curtains and counterpanes and, surprisingly, fashionable shoes! A more happy and most kindly communication goes to one who has just been chosen mother superior (when and of which house is not stated). She is urged to do, what indeed the bishop himself does, take a "positive" line in the exhortation of her nuns:

> . . . Do not say to a proud and haughty girl "You are proud and haughty" but rather, "My daughter be more humble. There is some appearance of pride in what you have said or done". And to an angry girl "Be more gentle . . . try to dominate anger".

Such rebukes, he argues, are the most efficacious in producing repentance. He adds, shrewdly as well as kindly, that thoughtful inquiries after those with poor health will enable them to make greater efforts than would otherwise be possible.

But the vials of wrath were emptied on all concerned on the day when an Ursuline took, from the lay viewpoint, an apparently blameless "day on the town" slipping out of the convent at 4 a.m. when the supplies were brought in for the day and, by permission of the bishop, returning under the somewhat grim escort of the chaplain, the Jesuit Father Glapion, to be received at the entrance by the superior, the portress and the *"zélatrice"* and conducted to her cell, where it would appear she was to remain for some time, her conversation restricted to the superior and the nun who brought her meals, neither of whom it may be supposed would be chatty. . . .

If Briand had a low opinion of himself there were some who unlike his friend Marchand had a low opinion of him. There was indeed a party in Quebec who apparently thought a bishop and the episcopal authority unnecessary and said so. Briand in some indignation sent off to Cardinal Castelli a list of epithets applied to him—"proud, distant, haughty, imperious, ambitious, choleric and passionate"; "hard and imperious". "Some of them have said that I was a protestant and that I was destroying religion. I have been told to my face that I was *"un chien de Breton entêté"*. His own people, he says, show him less respect than the English Protestants do.

Briand defended himself to the cardinal, referring to the diligence and simplicity of his life. "I confess that I am charged with sins before God, but not with scandalous faults". What is credible in the rather repetitious list of adjectives quoted is that Briand might be both choleric and stubborn. His "pride" boils down to a determination to hold together the church of which he was the unwilling bishop, to continue worship without persecution and to maintain the link with Rome. If he had pride, it was a very purposeful professional pride and it is clearly exhibited in his official policy.

First, there was to be no compromise. As bishop he was the father and the ruler of his flock standing in the place of Christ. Discipline, he reminded his people, had always been most rigid during times of persecution in the church. . . .

Although Briand would have agreed, and his letters show this, that his great task was to work within the church for order and discipline and zeal, he was always acutely conscious of the problem of relations with the secular power. If he welcomed the Quebec Act as an important victory, the attitude of many during the American invasion appeared to him a very dangerous reverse for his church. From the very beginning he had been quite clear on the duty of the habitant to the English government. He had taken the oath of allegiance; it must be kept. The English king was his ruler under God, and he must remember how fortunate he was to enjoy his religion under a government so strongly opposed to it. Those who supported the Americans disappointed and angered him. He was vigorous in urging his priests to recall the people to their duty, so much so that the habitants became a little bored with political sermons. In one of the parishes south of Quebec, as an obedient priest was expending himself in the good cause, some one at the back of the church shouted in tones of exasperation *"C'est assez prêcher pour les anglais!"* . . .

. . . Briand had to secure something beyond mere tolerance and independence for the church. In England as in France, church and state were linked together; they were two aspects of one society. On the one hand the Canadian church needed official recognition and countenance; by its very nature it demanded something beyond the bare toleration accorded to English Non-Conformists. It needed, for example, government countenance for public processions, for marriage usages, for all kinds of claims connected with property and civil rights. On the other hand, the British government needed an official church. In the absence of any system of public education or information the clergy were an essential element in maintaining among the people that unquestioning cooperation, docility and loyalty to established power which, however odious it may be to the modern mind, is still a humane and moral substitute for military terrorism and a secret police. It would be absurd to suggest that the vicar-general at Quebec saw all this clearly in 1763. But there seems to be no doubt that, astutely feeling his way, claiming where he could, yielding where he must anything permitted by conscience, he did in fact in twenty years establish his church effectively as the equivalent of the state church. If London knew him only as "the Superintendent of the Romish Religion", in Quebec, as I have said, he was the bishop to everyone from the governor down. When the first Anglican bishop arrived he found himself almost automatically with a denominational label, to him a position as odious as it was novel.

The victory, for it was a signal victory, was not achieved without difficulty. Murray, kind and generous to the nuns whom he liked and whose services he valued, undoubtedly took an Erastian or, perhaps one should say, an extremely Gallican view of the church. Briand learned not to announce the appointment of a priest, but to ask permission to appoint him; and to accept nominations of Murray which he disapproved, and with good reason; and even to give courteous explanations when Murray inquired into cases of ecclesiastical penalties such as refusal of the sacraments. But all this seems to have been not so much weakness as a careful calculation of what

might and therefore must be yielded. On one occasion, even as he yielded, he administered to Murray what, properly understood, could only have been taken as a rebuke. Murray had apparently requested temporary admission into a cloistered area for a Mlle. Desgoutins, and offered to pay for the privilege. Briand stated with great explicitness that such entry was forbidden by the rules and that to relax them for money would be a crime. "The wish of His Excellency is a more noble motive and more than sufficient and I make it my duty and honour to accord it."

In the matter of prayers in church for a heretic king, Briand had much searching of heart, and he yielded more than his colleagues at Montreal and Three Rivers and more than some in Quebec would have wished. He seems to have acted on principle and not from timidity. He could not find that the rules forbade public prayers for any not specifically excommunicated; it was proper to pray for the King; and the arguments pressed on him that it was hard to pray for one's enemies he decided, reasonably, were unacceptable. However, in requiring prayers for the monarch, he was careful to add no personal eulogy, and certainly no suggestion that his religious example was one to be followed.

But with all this apparent yielding no governor really got much beyond the church door. In the matter of refusal of sacraments: "I have had the honour to tell him [Murray] that neither I nor the Pope himself could do anything about refusal, delay or concession of absolution, because penitence was a secret and private tribunal whose judge would account only to God." His own power as bishop came to him not from the King but from the church. "What I have from the king is liberty and permission to exercise my ministry and use my powers."

Briand's reward for conciliation was the bishopric which he did not want. Much more, it was the appointment of a coadjutor to ensure the succession, a step authorized by Rome in 1766 but postponed for four long years in Quebec even by the obliging Governor Carleton. And it seems clear that here again Briand had to conciliate in practice in order to win in principle. A discreet attempt to find out who would be acceptable to the clergy in the district of Montreal offended the governor, and the man ultimately approved, or perhaps chosen, by Carleton was not the one Briand would have chosen. *"Le gouvernement a consenti à un coadjuteur et a paru désirer M. Desglis; je n'ai pas cru devoir m'y opposer; c'est un bon prêtre"*. Even the favoured M. Desglis was consecrated only after a "little storm" in which Catholics joined with Governor Carleton in urging that there was no need to wait for the papal bulls. This time however Briand did not yield. . . .

Marcel Trudel, "La Servitude de l'Église Catholique du Canada français sous le régime anglais", *Canadian Historical Association Report*, 1963, pp. 42-64. (Translated C.N.) Reprinted by permission of the Canadian Historical Association.

Servile

On the 10th of August 1764, there began for the Church of Canada a regime of servitude under a Protestant government. To be sure, the Church had already known servitude under a Catholic State: . . . However, this regime of servitude was a strength and a guarantee, for the Church depended on the Catholic king whose first duty was precisely to sustain and disseminate Catholicism throughout the world. Now this strength was to be transformed into a dramatic impotence, and this guarantee was to disappear when the rights of the Crown of France were ceded to the Crown of England.

Added to which, because of its lack of personnel, the Church in 1764 found itself in a most disquieting situation. It was a Church without a bishop; the Chapter had but five members in Canada, and these canons, a community of meditators, lived henceforth in a dispersed state; two great Orders—the Jesuits and the Recollets—no longer had the right to recruit members; the fate of the Sulpician community, formed of Frenchmen from

France, remained a long time in suspense; a community of women, that of the *Hôpital Général de Québec*, was on the verge of bankruptcy; another, that of the *Hôtel-Dieu de Montréal*, thought of returning to France. In five years the clergy had lost by death or desertion a quarter of its members; at the end of 1764 there were only 137 priests; there was still no bishop to perpetuate ordination, and clergy from France could no longer be counted upon. About the same time the Acadian Church died out. It is in this alarming context that the Catholic church not only fell under the domination of a Protestant king (who at his coronation had sworn to destroy Popery); but also (what had never been seen under the French regime), under the personal domination of the governors.

Without a doubt this Catholic church was to receive the support of the Protestant state. When the Church required a secular force to put its will into effect, the Protestant state was to furnish this force. . . .

This Church received as well the support of the Protestant government in the form of salaries given to Catholic missionaries among the Indians; and, especially, the most constant and weighty financial support furnished by the government went to the Episcopal Palace and the annual pension of the bishop. . . .

This financial support appeared for the first time in 1762, when Briand was still merely the Grand-Vicar of the Government of Quebec. Not being a member of any seminary nor of any order, holding only a meagre canonry and personally destitute, Briand had accepted from Governor Murray a present of twenty pounds sterling (being the equivalent of his canonry) "for his good behaviour." Made a bishop in 1766, he was assured of an annual pension of two hundred pounds sterling that the government called "a salary. . . . "

All this was to bring a very dangerous security to the Church. By permitting, and especially by asking, the Protestant state to serve as its secular arm, the state was brought to intervene in the private life of the Church. . . . Whether the gratuity came before or after, it remained nonetheless a means of binding the bishop to the interests of the government. . . .

The governor was not hesitant about calling for *mandements* and circular letters. Under the military regime, Gage in 1762 had wielded scissors of censorship upon an ecclesiastical *mandement*: under the English regime the governor intervened in just as encumbering a fashion. To invite the Canadians to repel the invaders, *Mgr*. Briand prepared a circular letter, but Carleton (whom he called "the most kindly of men, a charming man") demanded a *mandement* instead, and *Mgr*. Briand gave him satisfaction. By his circulars the bishop made himself in some ways the publicist, the *public crier*, of the government, which had never been done under the French regime, the dissemination of edicts and ordinances having been taken care of by the Captains of the Militia. In 1768 the bishop published a circular to make known the intentions of the government on the matter of taverns; in 1772, it was to inform the parishioners that it was illegal to give shelter to deserting soldiers. . . .

The Church also felt this servitude in the recruitment of members. In 1763 the king had decided to let the Jesuits and Recollets die out. The fate imposed on the Jesuits can easily be understood in the context of the period, the Jesuits being already persecuted and harried in Catholic countries, but why go after the Recollets? It seems as though England wanted thereby to reduce all the clergy to the secular condition, more immediately subject to the bishop, and more easily controllable. The government also wished to stop the entry of any new religious communities. . . .

The civil power also intervened with the *curés*. . . . It was Murray who first arrogated to himself, under the military regime, the right to intervene in the appointment to *curés,* and that, he wrote, "with a view to holding those *curés* in a state of necessary subjection. . . . "

Even if it intervened at one time or another in the nomination of *curés*, and though it subjected the *curés* to diverse civil tasks, the government had to leave the jurisdiction in this area to the bishop; it had more success in the episcopal domain. This occurred at the very beginning of the English regime. Convoked in utmost secrecy on September 15th 1763, the Chapter of Quebec elected as bishop the Sulpician Montgolfier, Superior of a rich community, an imposing man who could do without any aid from the state. A little later, Murray was named Governor-General, and he had his own candidate: the Grand-Vicar Briand, a timid man, without resources, attached to no community, and who had already received financial assistance from Murray. Because of the official opposition to him, Montgolfier withdrew; the canons proceeded to another election on the 11th of September 1764; they elected Briand. The English regime, barely a month old, had begun badly for the Catholic Church, the bishop of which was the choice of the English and Protestant governor. . . .

These . . . years of English servitude profoundly marked the Canadian Church of Quebec. First of all they Canadianized its episcopacy and its hierarchy. Because the state was opposed to the Church being directed by Europeans, Canadians gained access to the episcopate by 1770, something that had not occurred during the French regime. The Jesuits, all Frenchmen from France in 1760, were completely eliminated. The Seminary of Quebec, also composed in 1760 of French from France, was to seek recruits quite readily among the Canadians; as for the Seminary of Montreal, similarly composed of Frenchmen, it would end, in spite of itself and with interminable gnashing of teeth, by accepting Canadian Sulpicians. This Canadianization was not necessarily an advantage: the church renewed its resources in a closed environment, without being able to profit from the ideas of an outside world. . . .

In addition, it was the English regime which was to lead the Canadian Church into playing a rôle in society which was not strictly a spiritual one. . . . Under the English regime the Church became openly the vehicle for government orders; it took the census of human and material resources, it maintained the people in their allegiance to the Crown and (because the executive was linked to the Crown until 1848) in fidelity to the executive. . . . A spiritual power, the Church became a political power. . . .

Finally, the traditional Gallicanism of the Canadian Church was transformed into a ferocious Romanism. Gallican since the time of Mgr. de Saint-Vallier, the Canadian Church found itself in 1763 cut off from the sources of Gallicanism: the French secular clergy no longer furnished personnel, and the French episcopacy rapidly lost contact with the diocese of Quebec. . . .

Elizabeth Arthur, *Adam Mabane and the French Party in Canada,* (Montreal, McGill University, 1947), (unpublished M.A. thesis), pp. 40-41, 47-48. Reprinted by permission of the author.

The *Canadiens:*

More Catholic Than French

. . . By 1762, as well, Murray was differentiating between French and Canadian clergy . . . The Canadian clergy, Murray averred, had not the same feeling of attachment for France as had those born in that country. It is true that the joy Murray felt at this time at the news of increasing protests against the payment of tithes was quite inconsistent with the position later taken by the French party, as was Murray's hope that the Canadians might forsake their religion in favour of the English beliefs, but the explanation of this apparent inconsistency lies in the party struggles that followed 1763. Out of those struggles emerged one party dedicated to the conservation of things Canadian, and another equally dedicated to the advancement of commercial interests. So sharp was the cleavage between them that the French party abandoned certain of its early prejudices, and henceforth supported wholeheartedly the project of returning to the old laws and customs of the country.

Even before Murray was forced to abandon his belief that the simple expedient of leaving the Canadians without a bishop might slowly induce them to forsake their religion, he realized quite clearly that any such change would not come quickly. He stressed the necessity of quieting Canadian fears over the fate of the Roman Catholic church in Canada, and advised the continuance of the communities of women (although no protests could convince him that Recollets or Jesuits should remain). In addition, he tried to secure government help in rebuilding the parish church at Quebec. There is some evidence that Murray, at this period, sought to reassure the Canadians in their religion, and at the same time envisaged a day when their religion would be far from secure; yet it is doubtful that he ever was conscious of this inconsistency. . . .

. . . Murray, for political reasons, forsook the idea of a Protestant Canada, and in the course of time it became increasingly evident that Roubaud [the ex-Jesuit and secret British agent] was not to be trusted, and that his schemes were usually for personal gain rather than public good, so that the danger-period for the Roman Catholic faith passed quickly. For a brief time, however, it did appear that [in the words of Thomas Chapais] *"les infiltrations protestantes gagnant de proche en proche . . . le peuple canadien glisserait insensiblement du catholicisme à l'anglicanisme et de l'anglicanisme à l'anglicisation."*

In 1763, hopes for the eventual anglicization of the inhabitants had dictated the policy laid down explicitly in Murray's instructions. He was not to permit "any ecclesiastical jurisdiction of the See of Rome or of any other foreign ecclesiastical jurisdiction whatever," but three years later considerations of political expediency, the danger of creating any abiding sense of grievance in Canada, the apparent safety of entrusting Briand with power, and Murray's own reliance upon support from the Canadians, led to the almost furtive consecration of Briand as Bishop of Quebec in a chapel outside Paris in March, 1766.

It was in no spirit of jubilation that the new bishop prepared to return to Canada; his fears for his religion were still acute, for he saw in England how precarious Murray's position really was, and there was as yet no indication that the French party in Canada could survive the governor's recall. Briand's fears may have been in some part allayed by the reception given him upon his return to Quebec, for the public demonstration was not exclusively French-Canadian; the entire population had some cause for rejoicing, because those who could not greet the appearance of a Roman Catholic bishop with anything but apprehension could celebrate the departure of Murray for England to answer to the accusations against him. The same issue of the Quebec Gazette carried both stories, and it must have been difficult to determine over which event each individual was rejoicing.

Although Murray, to whom in great part the victory for Roman Catholicism was due, could not be present to greet the new Bishop, he left him a letter expressing his congratulations, confiding the Canadians to his care, and assuring Briand that Mabane would do everything possible to smooth his path. It was in a burst of good feeling among the French-Canadians, both lay and clerical, that Murray left Canada, and it is impossible to say how much his reputation has gained by this coincidence. Behind him he left a multitude of disputes, but one alliance firmly fixed—that between the Canadians and the French party. From Rome came the advice that the Canadians should be most discreet, most expressive of their gratitude toward those who had secured this favour for them: *"ils doivent oublier à cet égard, qu'ils sont Français."* Likewise, the position of the French party was clearly laid down: friendship with the leaders of the Roman Catholic church and protection of the Roman Catholic faith were essential first principles.

Part VI

A New Broom:
Carleton

The imperial authorities, in a manner reminiscent of the old masters of Quebec, had a simple solution to colonial problems: they recalled the governor. This was the fate of James Murray. The authorities had had many complaints of the evil administration of the good governor: his authoritarianism; his refusal to implement the Proclamation, and in particular his refusal to call an assembly; his nepotism and favouritism. Not only was he recalled, but his regime was investigated.

Guy Carleton replaced Murray. In many ways the new governor was a replica of the old: at first only in temperament, afterwards in policy as well. But his early days in the colony, as Arthur points out, were partly devoted to undoing Murray's policies. He was a new broom. Soon, however, he was to change his views. The ineffective Royal Proclamation staggered along. In 1770, Carleton returned to England, and by 1774 Murray's policies were fully confirmed in the Quebec Act.

R. H. Mahon, *Life of the Hon. James Murray: a Builder of Canada*, (London, John Murray, 1921), pp. 342-373. Reprinted by permission of John Murray (Publishers) Ltd., London.

Alas,

Poor Murray

. . . On October 18, 1765, the Lords of the Privy Council considered the case of Mr. Thomas Walker and the civil and military discord that reigned in Canada, and in consequence of their representations to the King the following letter, dated October 24, 1765, was addressed to Governor Murray:

"SIR,—Divers representations having been made to His Majesty in council of the disorders that have lately happened and the unfortunate divisions reigning in the province of Quebec, where you command, I am in consequence of the same to signify to you His Majesty's pleasure that you do immediately prepare for your return to England, in order to give a full and distinct account of the present state of the said province, of the nature and causes of the disorders and divisions above mentioned, and of your own conduct and proceedings in the administration of your Government.

"It is, however, His Majesty's pleasure you should not leave the province till you receive His Majesty's further orders, and till a proper person shall be fixed on by His Majesty for the government of the province during your absence. . . ."

Quite apart from the strong suspicion that the Rockingham Ministry were guilty of weak concession to the pressure of public clamour of an obviously biassed nature, it was surely impolitic thus to weaken the authority of the Governor of Quebec at a time when it was all important that strong government should be supported by every possible means. The immediate effect of this mandate was to enable Walker and the recalcitrant traders to declare that the recall of the Governor was due to their representations, and to argue therefrom that the Government at home viewed with favour the principles of their agitation. Such an outcome was not only a serious incentive to the spirit of rebellion, which was already in evidence in the neighbouring states, but it also tended to undermine the whole structure of loyalty among the French Canadians, which Murray had so assiduously developed. They could not but argue that the recall of a man in whom they trusted, apparently at the behest of a small number of British subjects, from which they had every reason to expect injustice and oppression, indicated that the policy of the conqueror was undergoing a change. It would even appear that Walker, who went to England to lay his grievances in person before Lord Dartmouth, was informed of the recall of the Governor before Murray himself:

"I am far from doubting the recall," writes Murray to the Lords of Trade, "but I must lament that Mr. Walker should have known it before I did, and that some clerks of the offices should have communicated to him what he had no right to know. I should be defective in my duties was I not to acquaint Lord Dartmouth that Mr. Walker takes uncommon liberties with his name. Nothing can be more ridiculous to men of sense, but in a colony constituted as this is the mischief may be irreparable, unless a stop be put to the mercenary agent's career. He does not hesitate to say that he is protected by the King's servants in stirring up the people to spurn at every ordinance and regulation made by the Governor of the province. . . . I shall not, however, be deterred from doing my duty . . . the murmurs of a few British traders residing here I must expect until I can convince the colony that my letters are read at the Board of Trade with as much attention as Mr. Walker's remonstrances."

Moreover, the means to acquaint themselves of all the circumstances of the disorders which had occurred were already in the hands of the Board of Trade. Cramahé, who besides being Murray's secretary, was also a member of the council, had been sent to England for the express purpose of laying before the ministers the state of the case. Mr. Price, also a member of the council, had been sent shortly after the great fire, which had destroyed a considerable part of the town of Montreal, to seek aid for the sufferers, and he too would be in a position to give information. That Conway, in his capacity of Secretary of State, should have signed the letter of recall to Murray had in itself a special degree of irony, for Conway was honest and the consistent opponent of oppression in the American colonies. He was, moreover, a soldier, and had no sympathy with demagogues, whether Wilkes or Walker. He had warmly denied Pitt's general accusation against the Ministry, and declared that he at least "had not made use of liberty to ride into employment." Indeed this parrot cry of liberty had brought with it ill-fortune for Murray, for we have seen that under one Ministry he had had neglect because the Westminster mob had howled themselves hoarse for "Murray and liberty," and the sins of the brother had been visited on him, and now for the opposite reason

"Wilkes and liberty" had a sinister effect on his career from a Ministry anxious to conciliate the people.

It is convenient here to anticipate events by a few months, in order to describe the outcome of the agitation created in Canada by the disappointed British merchants and fostered by their representatives in London. In July, 1766, the Rockingham Ministry fell, the cause being the repeal of the American Stamp Act, which Horace Walpole tells us was forced by the "clamour of trade, of the merchants, and of the manufacturing towns." "Trade" saw in the positive intention of the colonists to cease all trading until their claims had been satisfied, an endless series of losses which to the merchants was of more importance than any question of political loss which might ensue from hasty legislation. This very Government, forced by one section of trade to act unjustly to the hero of this memoir, was forced to repeal the Stamp Act by another section, and thus to set themselves in opposition to the King and the Court party, which promptly commenced to plot their downfall. By July, 1766, the King had sent for Mr. Pitt, and as Earl of Chatham a new Government had been brought together under his leadership.

It is not relevant to this story to dilate upon the extraordinary state of the political world, which was at this time a chaos of individuals, each playing a personal game and no one giving more than a passing thought to the condition of the country, or the great interests at stake. Horace Walpole, for all that he records his part as the *Deus ex Machina*, who brought the wandering atoms together in ever changing groups, and uses the personal pronoun with irritating frequency, makes it clear that in such a state of ill-defined political thought it would be impossible to find unanimity in any one party. There was in practice no Ministry and no Opposition, for within the Ministry were opposing factions, and without it were those who supported one section or another of the cabinet itself; the result tended to form unstable groups, which, like so many chemical combinations, contained the principles of explosion, and explosion was not infrequently the result. . . .

Murray arrived in England at the end of July, 1766, to answer before a hostile Ministry the ridiculous charges brought against him by the discontented traders of Quebec—persons who he described as "the most immoral collection of men I ever knew." It is unnecessary to waste much time over the "charges" which appeared to Lord Dartmouth a sufficient reason to recall a Governor in whose favour petitions from all the most respectable members of the community poured in. All of these petitions struck one key-note.

"We pray your Majesty, if you will deign to listen to us, continue Monsr. Murray as Governor of this province, which his valour has preserved for you, and who has gained the affection of its people by his generosity and mildness, and restore him to us." And again, "We dare to hope that he will be continued in that office, where his enlightened mind and equity and prudence enable him to keep the people in a state of tranquility and obedience."

Fortunately his arrival in England synchronised with the fall of the Rockingham Ministry, but the new Ministry, which included Lord Shelburne as Secretary of State, with Colonel Barré as a privy councillor holding office as Vice-Treasurer for Ireland, and Lord Hills-

borough, whose peculiar notions of the interpretation of the King's Proclamation in Canada have already been noticed, as President of the Board of Trade, were unlikely to be favourable to him. Nevertheless, if he could not expect sympathy and support, the new Ministry was, at least, more honest than their predecessors, and an honest inquiry was what Murray earnestly desired.

"The charges" were obviously framed to please the narrow religious views of Dartmouth, and to most of them Murray replied with scathing contempt. Accused of giving away the brandy found in the French king's stores at Quebec, he replied:

"I gave the brandy for intelligence; no man ever had better (*i.e.*, during the campaign of 1760). I am sure nobody ever wanted it more, and that no nation ever paid less for it. So I displeased the little Protestant traders. . . . Quakers, Puritans, Anabaptists, Presbyterians, Atheists, Infidels, and even Jews."

Then with a touch that reminds one of Warren Hastings at a later date, he exclaimed: "Had avarice been my passion it might have been gratified without robbing the King of eight thousand gallons of brandy." Enacting ordinances "injurious to civil liberty and the Protestant cause," "Encouraging your Majesty's new subjects to apply for judges of their own national language," "Leaving the Protestants to this day destitute of a place of worship appropriated to themselves," were items among the "charges."

One stands astonished that any responsible statesman should have been unable to see through such trash, and much more not worth quoting; but so far as Murray was concerned, the indictment must have occasioned much anxiety and labour, and it was not until April following (1767) that the Privy Council dismissed the several complaints, as we have already seen, as "groundless, scandalous, and derogatory to the honour of the said Governor, who stood before the committee unimpeached."

Elizabeth Arthur, *Adam Mabane and the French Party in Canada*, (Montreal, McGill University, 1947), unpublished M.A. thesis, pp. 92-95. Reprinted by permission of the Author.

Carleton Equals

Murray?

. . . , Carleton, at the time he came to Canada, did not share the ideas of the French party, and even if Mabane and Irving had continued as members of his Council, it is not likely that they would have enjoyed his confidence. He came to the colony resolved to watch the Canadians narrowly for any signs of sympathy with the French, whom he considered to be England's natural enemies; he had not yet come to regard the *noblesse* with admiration, nor had he discovered in 1766 that the Roman Catholic church deserved his protection. He was still much influenced by his attorney-general, Francis Maseres—a descendent of Huguenots who had fled from France after the revocation of the Edict of Nantes, and hence rabidly anti-Catholic. Both Maseres and William Hey, the new Chief Justice, were able men; both were friends of Fowler Walker, the London attorney who had represented the Canadian merchants in their attacks upon Murray; both were inclined to favour the mercantile group. It is true that in the course of time Carleton developed very different ideas, but there is nothing to suggest that his position in 1766 was such that, provided they were sufficiently agreeable, he would seize upon Mabane and Irving as his natural allies.

. . . Carleton seems to have decided that the best way to quell the Canadian tumults and also to ingratiate himself with the home government, was to make his predecessors' actions appear in the worst possible light. Even in small matters he contrived to disparage Murray wherever possible. For example, he gave a pension to the son of the Captain Nadeau whom Murray had ordered hanged in 1760 for supplying food to the French army, contrary to orders. Maseres, still in Carleton's favour at this time, railed against Murray, whose acquittal he considered a conviction in the eyes of all impartial men, and denied that the governor had really been well thought of by the Canadians. In addition, Carleton's renunciation of the fees of office immediately upon his arrival tended to suggest that the previous governor had been avaricious. It is quite true that the whole fee system was in need of reform, but the timing of the change was such that it threw reflections upon the governor personally. Murray answered these suggestions in an article in Lloyd's Evening Post, January 25, 1767, but it is unlikely that many people in Canada ever saw it. The merchants who did have access to English newspapers would not circulate it, and Carleton's council had been purged of most of its pro-Murray members before the letter was considered in May of the same year. Laying the letter before the council was not likely to raise any storm by that time, and inclusion of Murray's defence in the minutes was an extremely shrewd move on Carleton's part. There it would be read by the appropriate Secretary of State in London, and it could be used to emphasize the impression of fairness which Carleton was seeking to create there.

Carleton was certainly too much of a politician to align himself with the men who had been unalterably attached to Murray, even if they had shown any disposition to cooperate with him. Instead, he began his career in Canada by showing favour to those who had abused Murray most heartily, and gave appointments to Murray's enemies in the hope of appeasing them. He had come endowed with the combined civil and military powers for which Murray had pleaded in vain, and he sought to end the divisions within the colony. In such a policy, the leaders of the party which had formerly ruled Canada would be a hindrance rather than a help. To be sure, it became evident in time that choosing officials on the basis of their disapproval of his predecessor was not altogether reliable, and even Maseres soon discovered that George Allsopp—to whom he had been drawn at first—was chiefly remarkable for his ability to instigate quarrels. "He made it the business of his life to revile and defame Governor Murray and the members of his Council in a most licentious and illiberal manner."

Part VII

The Conquest:
Nationalism and/or
Separatism?

We began with the general question: what happens when a country is conquered? The question, as it related to the former colony of New France, has been answered in part. The problem, however, concerns not only what happened years ago but relates to what is occurring today. The early years of the British regime, 1759 to 1766, are remote from us, but their significance for Canadian and *Canadien* society continues to be discussed and passionately debated in the current historical literature.

The real significance of the Conquest, not unnaturally, is disputed mainly by *Canadien* historians, and in particular by Fernand Ouellet and Michel Brunet. When the controversy began, the former was a member of the *Institut d'histoire* at *l'Université Laval* and the latter was a member of the History Department at the *Université de Montréal*. These French-language universities are still the fountainheads of the two opposing views on the ultimate significance of the Conquest for the French Canadians.

The original source of the controversy, however, is neither Ouellet nor Brunet, but Maurice Séguin, a colleague of Brunet; his ideas have deeply influenced his colleagues and students. To Séguin, *nationalism* and *separatism* are linked; the history of Quebec and Canada is dominated, in his opinion, by the national struggle, what Durham called "two nations warring in the bosom of a single state." He sees no harm in the colonial relationship of New France to France, in fact he calls it separatism. But the Conquest, although still representing a colonial link, is a bad thing.

Ouellet's piece, entitled "Is Nationalism Dispensable?" challenges the whole base of the Séguin-Brunet argument. If nationalism did not exist in New France how could the Conquest have created a national struggle? Further, the subsequent condition of Quebec is not the result of the Conquest, but rather of the unwillingness of the *Canadiens* to abandon a misguided and archaic ideology. Philippe Garigue, the Dean of the Social Sciences at the *Université de Montréal*, and an adherent of the Séguin hypothesis, contradicts Ouellet. He defines the constituent elements of a national group, examines the society of New France and Quebec, and concludes that the society was and is a viable national entity.

Michel Brunet's two selections examine, specifically and generally, the effects of a conquest on a society. The displacement of the economic elite of New France through emigration, or through inability to raise capital, left the society of Quebec with a dearth of leadership. This decapitation of the French elite did not lead to the death of *Canadien* society, for direction was still given by its replacement, the British head. The result, however, was to place the French Canadians in positions of inferiority. The *Canadiens* lost political and economic dominance to the British. This in turn led them, for the sake of survival, to emphasize forms of activity which differed and differentiated them from the British, what Brunet in another essay has called "*Les trois dominantes de la pensée canadienne-française: l'agriculturisme, l'anti-étatisme et le messianisme.*"[1] His synonym for these patterns is the word "myths." Brunet's writings blend many disciplines: history, sociology, economics and psychology. He resorts to this last when he asserts that lack of opportunities in the political and economic spheres deprived the French Canadians of the ability to act, and this then became enshrined as a cultural norm,

where it acted as a barrier to change. All these ills according to Brunet, flow from the conquest of New France.

Jean Hamelin contradicts Michel Brunet. The whole of what is called the *Conquest Hypothesis* is invalid for the good and simple reason that its historical basis, the French regime, has been distorted. There was no significant economic elite in New France. On the contrary, the ideology which dominated the Old Regime, used in a very pejorative sense, was retrogressive. Ouellet, the chief spokesman of the Anti-Conquest Hypothesis historians, is presented in the last selection by means of a historiographical essay. Serge Gagnon's article presents the interpretations current at the *Université de Montréal* and at *l'Université Laval*. The part here quoted deals specifically with the many writings of Fernand Ouellet. Underlying Ouellet's views, in addition to historical evidence, is a psychological interpretation of social classes. Ouellet emphasizes the lack of bourgeois mentality, of that essential "spirit of capitalism." It is this, and not nationalism, that might be the salvation of French Canada.

The issues raised by these controversialists are germane to contemporary problems. If Séguin, Brunet and Garigue are correct in their interpretations of the French regime, the Conquest, and subsequent developments, then it follows that, to secure her full national identity, Quebec would have to separate. Otherwise French Canada is doomed at best to a marginal existence, at worst to assimilation in an Anglo-American sea. If Ouellet is correct, separatism, today as in the past, would merely enshrine false ideologies and create more problems than it would solve. The former group implies that it is impossible to be a French Canadian and a Canadian at the same time; Ouellet that there is a single valid Canadian condition for all.

---

[1]—Michel Brunet, "Les trois dominantes de la pensée canadienne-française", in La Présence Anglaise et les Canadiens, pp. 113-166.

Maurice Séguin, "Genèse et historique de l'idée séparatiste au Canada français", (*Laurentie*, juin 1962), pp. 965-968. (Translated C.N.). Reprinted by permission of the author.

Separatism

From the point of view of the *independantiste*, the situation of Canada in the French empire is not a subject for idealization but rather for re-evaluation. It is the only epoch in our history when separatism was rooted in reality. For over a hundred years the Canadians of French origin lived alone in a separate state. They defended this separatism even by force of arms, without inclining to any federalist doctrine, and without attempting to become a minority in a greater whole dominated by a foreign nation.

As long as French Canada remained alone, as long as the reasons for its birth and for its growth as a people [continued], the metropolitan state sustained it, protecting it from a military point of view, colonizing it with her sons, her institutions, her capital resources. As long as these conditions existed it was in a position to become a normal nation. When Canada realized its weaknesses and the preponderance of English forces over the French in America, it did not turn to an alliance or a federation that would have meant annexation to the stronger British colonies, but rather it turned to

its mother country and requested more colonists, more capital, or better protection.

Immediately after the Anglo-American conquest the little French Canadian population of sixty thousand souls could have been dragged into the orbit of the English population of America, a million and a half strong. The territory of Quebec, invaded by an English minority, could have been annexed to the greater foreign entity which could have federated into a single British North-American nation. This evolution would have rapidly settled the political fate of French Canada. It would have been clearly annexed to English America without being able to play off one group of Anglo-Americans against another group of Anglo-Americans. But the conquest of Canada was followed immediately by an emancipation crisis of the old colonies, the unity of British America could not develop, and the great schism in Anglo-Saxon America artificially divided English America into two systems. . . .

Thus twice in the first thirty years after the Conquest French Canada escaped the centralization of a federal regime and annexation to a greater English America: . . . A whole series of circumstances conjoined to assist the cause of the French Canadians. All these events seemed to furnish the French Canadians with possibilities for political re-conquest.

But warnings were not lacking: warnings given as early as 1763 by the Colonial Office [*sic*] which was aware of the grave problem that would be posed [because of] the French Canadians being in a majority, in spite of the . . . efforts of the English population to establish themselves in Canada; a warning repeated in 1766 by a high official who, foreseeing the difficulties which an English population would have to become a majority in Canada, did not want to see these difficulties increased and the assimilation of the French Canadians made impossible by the granting of an assembly dominated by the French Canadians; warnings understood by the Imperial Government which had the wisdom, in 1774, to refuse an assembly because it gave too many powers to the French Canadians. . . .

Fernand Ouellet, "Le Nationalisme Canadien-français: de ses origines à l'insurection de 1837", *Canadian Historical Review*, Volume XLV, 1964, pp. 277-292. (Translated C.N.) Reprinted by permission of the University of Toronto Press.

Is Nationalism Dispensable?

Viewed in the light of traditional historiography, and even from the viewpoint of the neo-nationalist, the problem of the origins of French Canadian nationalism would be easy to resolve. In effect, the nationalist historians of Quebec have held the conviction that the national framework is indispensable to any collective existence. That is why they have affirmed, without a shadow of doubt, that the birth of French Canadian nationalism dated from the origins of New France. This thesis, hardly contested until very recently though highly controversial, we find clearly exposed in Guy Frégault's book, *"La Civilization de la Nouvelle-France."* The inhabitants of the Laurentian Valley, affirms this historian, had a sense of their "ethnic individuality" from the seventeenth century, and, a century later, they had a true "national consciousness." One can understand the significance of this interpretation. Here the essential foundations of the *drama of the*

Conquest and its tragic consequences are outlined.

For most nationalist historians, it is the struggle for survival immediately after 1760 that attracts them, a struggle that was not and is never to stop; for others, the Conquest inaugurated the period of great displacements and sterile compromises. The vision of Canon Groulx, based on past victories and past roots, begins with the battle for survival and the no less glorious constitutional struggles. . . . On the other hand the perception of Michel Brunet, who rejects the "mythification of the past," rests on the representation of the cataclysm of the Conquest which, according to him, by decapitating the French Canadian nation of its bourgeoisie, doomed the young nation to inferiority and degeneration. According to Brunet and Séguin, it was only social decapitation that reduced the French Canadians to a state of servitude; the drama of the Conquest, by severing every tie with the former mother-country, had a traumatic effect on that fragile entity that was the Canadian nation. . . . Thus, between the comforting positions of Canon Groulx and the pessimism of Mr. Michel Brunet, we note, in spite of some appreciable differences, a common point of departure: namely, the existence before 1760 of a French Canadian nation. Their entire interpretations of Canadian history follow logically from this first affirmation and from the particular conception they hold of the character of that nationality. . . .

The Conquest did not engender any essential change in the life of the inhabitant of the Laurentian valley. It even, by eliminating the profiteers of the old system, clarified many situations and benefitted a number of merchants. . . . Immediately after 1760, the citizen of New France is not a being whose psychological buoyancy has been shattered and whose single destination is bondage. Fruitful perspectives open before him, multiple choices are evident in the challenges that bring themselves to his attention. His fate thus is related to the quality of his responses.

Under these conditions, it would be difficult to explain why the Conquest should have unleashed the famous struggle for survival, or the deterioration of French Canadian society. Between 1760 and 1791 there existed conflicts, but these had no national character. They were, properly speaking, social, and placed the governors, administrators and *seigneurs* of all origins in opposition to the commercial classes. At this period the fundamental cleavage was not as yet ethnic but social. . . .

In reality the nationalist interpretation lives on mere abstractions and projections; it is based on facts but, without meaning to do so, it exaggerates and deforms their significance. Thus the policy expressed in the Royal Proclamation of 1763 was credited with being the major incident that stimulated the defensive reflexes of the elite of the French Canadian nation. If this were so, the clergy and the *seigneurs* would have assumed the leadership of the masses in the struggle for survival and, thanks to the support of good governors, forced the leaders of London to revise their positions. That conception at the outset is in error regarding the real meaning of the policy adopted in 1763; it confuses traditionalism with nationalism and is singularly mistaken about the course of events during the period.

The policy that the English leaders attempted to apply in 1763 had not been elaborated with the goal of subjecting the French Canadian majority to a British minority. For its point of departure, it rested rather on a double expectation. Its promoters believed that the new regime would inaugurate an era of unprecedented prosperity out of which in a few years would emerge a type of "mercantile" society dominated by the bourgeoisie. They had, besides, the conviction that, thanks to the institutional changes and this new economic context, the colony would see a massive immigration which would give the British a numerical preponderance in a short while. These expectations belonged more to the realm of dreams than reality.

Very speedily it became evident that the course of events would be altogether different. From this point of view the crises of 1765-1766 had a salutary effect. The government leaders and many others realized before long that they could not hope for any major changes in the economic structure. As for immigration, it was realized after a few years of observation that its future was not very promising.

This series of events, unfavourable to the hopes for assimilation [held by the promoters of the policy], signifies, especially at a time when the revolutionary agitation took shape in New England, that the new regime had henceforth to base its social structures and its institutions on the French Canadian majority. . . . From then on, there would be no question of imposing on the French Canadians institutions that would conform to the ambitions of bourgeois capitalism and to British traditions. One can understand why the policy of 1763 began to disintegrate after it had barely been instituted. In this perspective, the Quebec Act appears as the sanctification of that evolution, and not as the initiation of a new order of things. . . .

Philippe Garigue, *L'Option Politique du Canada Français: une Interpretation de la Survivance Nationale,* (Montreal, Editions du Lévrier, 1963), pp. 7, 9-10, 13-14, 16, 27-29, 40, 51, 57-58, 123. (Translated C.N.) Reprinted by permission of the author.

Nationalism is

Indispensable

FOREWORD

. . . It is not the purpose of this book to furnish a total explanation of French Canada. Its objective is more limited, less ambitious. We have sought as a sociologist to study French Canada, and outline an appreciation which, without being a judgment of the whole, would convey an explanation of certain aspects of French Canadian behaviour.

All the possible reasons suggested as obstructions to normal development appear to have been mentioned—the conquest of 1760, the "colonial" situation of French Canada, the weakness of the educational system, the orientation of social values, the "domination" of the Catholic clergy, the "peasant" atavism of the French Canadians, the apathy of the population and the fear of innovations, the lack of "democratic" thought, the antagonism and the discrimination of English-speaking Canadians, etc.

. . . However, in spite of the impossibility of accepting any of these generalizations as the prime and fundamental cause of the delay in the development of French Canada, there can be no doubt that each possesses an explanatory element. The conquest of 1760 was the cause of a social disintegration. The French Canadians were treated as a "conquered" people. The educational system was not only badly oriented, but was inadequate for the needs of the group, etc. Consequently, the most rapid examination reveals not only the reality of the situation that each of these generalizations seeks to explain, but also the existence of a certain degree of causality. . . .

Presented in such fashion, it becomes possible to undertake the sociological analysis of French Canada as an inquiry into an explanatory cause for the continuance of factors unfavourable to its development. The interest of our study is, therefore, first of all methodological. It is an exercise in what researchers call the localization of the "variable strategic determinant."

THEORETICAL INTRODUCTION

. . . According to our conception, the problem posed by the analysis of French Canada belongs in the category of sociological analysis known as "analysis of total societies." This type of analysis emphasizes the structural, functional, integrative and disintegrative factors of vast social groupings. But these social groupings do not all possess the same general characteristics or even the same level of organization. . . .

Arbitrarily, but with some justification obtained by a summary examination, it is possible to say that French Canada constitutes an ethnic, linguistic, and even a cultural group, since the majority of people who call themselves French Canadians are the descendants of the inhabitants of New France, speak French, and identify themselves with symbols and values that distinguish them from members of other Canadian groups. . . .

Sociologically, if we accept the idea that the nation is an organizational projection of the continuity of the idea of the cultural grouping, it is in the attitudes of the members towards this grouping that we find the existence of a nation. It is the presence of certain cultural norms—like the preference for a common outlook, a will to continue to make the most of the presence of the group, the development of symbols and of collective representations, etc.—that permit the observer to verify the existence of the nation. . . .

TO EXIST IS TO SURVIVE

In choosing the concept of survival as a working hypothesis for the analysis, we do more than direct a sociological interpretation. We consider that the notion of survival is also the principal element of social adhesion of French Canada, and of its cultural "ethos." For it seems to us that the notion of survival, the inner coherence of French Canadian culture, is also that of the perception of social reality. The interlacing of natural time and of historical time has produced among the French Canadians a special dimension of duration and of existence. The temporality of French Canada in its three dimensions of past, present, and future is not, in the perception of the French Canadians, a succession of unrelated stages, but the result of a survival, of a will to being. . . .

THE NOTION OF SURVIVAL FROM 1760 TO CONFEDERATION

The first reaction of the French Canadians to the conquest of 1760 was a passive one. Their submission is ren-

dered acceptable by their discouragement over the defeat, and the benevolent actions of the conquerors. The military regime from 1759 to 1764 is often described as being more acceptable to the Canadians than that of the representatives of the King of France. Gradually the passive phase was transformed into a consent which, if not general, is very widespread:

They say of me, and they say of you, that I am English, indeed, you should be: they [les Canadiens] should also be; as they have taken the oath for it and all the natural laws, divine, human, impose it upon them. But neither I, nor you, nor they, ought to be of the English religion. What the poor people do not understand is [that] they are under English domination in civil matters.

This passage from a letter of Monseigneur Briand clearly indicates the emotional attitude of a large number of French Canadians, as well as the preoccupations of the ecclesiastic authorities. These last directed their official actions primarily towards the survival of the Catholic Church. It is possible to say that at this time one of the aspects of the notion of survival was born: the idea that the continuity of one of the characteristics of the group permitted the continuity of the group. . . .

THE FOUNDATIONS OF NATIONAL LEGITIMACY

. . . In the case of French Canada the vast majority of the social conditions of New France appear to have led the colony towards the creation of particularisms. The application of such a sociological pattern therefore suggests that well before 1760 French Canadian society, in that it had developed the principal elements of its social life, had laid the basis of a new cultural identity and thus of a national legitimacy. This hypothesis raises the problem of measuring the extent of the transformations that made it a distinct society and that, after 1760, legalized the national continuity of French Canada.

. . . It would seem that after the Conquest the French Canadians entered a phase of "sociological displacement" in their attitudes and their cultural values. This displacement occurred on several levels, . . . first, the development of a defensive consciousness by which the French Canadians became aware that their grouping was a form of security, an opportunity of assuring their survival; and then, a refusal of what is called "assimilation," and is the equivalent of opposing themselves to the social and cultural characteristics of the dominant English group. In effect, opposition to assimilation exists as early as the conquest of 1760, and the cultural conflict was rapidly "institutionalized. . . ."

IDEOLOGY AND ALIENATION

As we have pointed out in the pre-

ceding chapters, the development of the French Canadian consciousness is the consequence of developments through which the national characteristics of the group became precise. But in spite of a fundamental continuity, these developments are often in conflict, giving rise to a diversification of the elements of French Canadian identity. Each stage in the elaboration of the French Canadian nation is, therefore, in a sense, provisional. . . .

Analysis has shown us that successively, and as early as New France, profound differences influenced behaviour. After 1760 there is a discontinuity between institutions, and in spite of the rôle of nationalism as an ideological integrator, differing orientations were institutionalized in French Canadian thought. Thus even at the heart of the nationalism it is possible to differentiate between a national-catholicism and an unhyphenated nationalism, that is to say political nationalism. . . .

Michel Brunet, "La Conquête anglaise et la déchéance de la bourgeoisie canadienne" (1760-1793), *La Présence Anglaise et les Canadiens*, (Montréal, Beauchemin, 1958), pp. 49-57, 112. (Translated C.N.) Reprinted by permission of the author.

The Decapitation of

Canadien Society

New France had had its bourgeoisie. These men occupied posts of control in commerce, industry, in the army and in the administration. It was composed of nobles and plebeians, of Frenchmen and of *Canadiens*. The creation and expansion of the French empire in America cannot be explained without the presence of a managerial class interested in exploiting the riches of the continent...

In 1760, therefore, Canada included, as did all Western societies that evolved under normal conditions, a secular leading class comprised of administrators, soldiers, and businessmen. This elite, to which it would be an exaggeration, perhaps, to give the name of upper bourgeoisie, nonetheless met the requirements of a modest colonial society of some 60,000 inhabitants. It furnished the necessary framework. With the passing years, this naturally ambitious elite would have grown and would have played a more and more important rôle in the development

of the country. The Conquest determined otherwise.

Because of the Conquest and its aftermath, what was the fate of this *Canadien* bourgeoisie? This question has stirred up numerous discussions, and even some polemic. These last originate from a misunderstanding born of imprecise and incomplete data. The aim of this study is to bring out some particulars to show how the vanquished of 1760 lost their bourgeoisie.

The first French Canadian historians, Michel Bibaud, F.-X. Garneau and J.-B.-A. Ferland, have stated that to a certain degree their compatriots did not possess, as did other nations whose historical evolution had not experienced any irreparable disruption, an elite of businessmen, statesmen, administrators, intellectuals and scholars. In a word, a bourgeoisie ...

These historians and their successors, as well as outsiders who have studied the history of French Canada since the English Conquest, are unanimous, for example, in emphasizing the prominent rôle that the clergy played in Canadian society after 1760. The Church, however, had never occupied so important a place in the time of New France, particularly from the end of the seventeenth century. At that time the colony had its lay leadership. Historians, sociologists and observers, not having pursued their inquiries further, have not explained why the conquered *Canadiens* had to depend almost exclusively upon their priests to furnish them with a framework of leadership so necessary to human society, an improvised and necessarily incomplete framework. What had happened to the lay leadership of the Canadian society? ...

In 1899, Judge Louis-François-Georges Baby published a well-researched study in which he showed, with statistics, that there had not been a massive emigration of the managerial classes. Since then it has been repeated with a sigh of relief that the Conquest did not deprive the *Canadiens* of their natural leaders.

Unfortunately this comforting affirmation has closed our eyes to the distressing fate of the *Canadien* bourgeoisie after the Conquest. Did the natural leaders of the Canadian people have the liberty fully to fulfil their rôle? Did not the Conquest reduce their number? Did it not relegate them to an inferior rôle? These are the questions that we must ask ourselves before we can assert that the conquered *Canadiens* retained their social patterns.

Even if the emigration was not massive, it did considerably reduce the numbers of the leading families. The French administrators returned to the metropolis. How many of them would have remained in Canada if the country had remained a French colony? It is impossible to answer this question. But we do know that French families who came to the colony on official missions often decided to remain. . . .

Among the Canadian elite it appears that the merchants were those who held the greatest illusions. They even saw in the Conquest a genuine benefit. To understand this somewhat surprising reaction, it must be remembered that the businessmen who remained in the country were drawn from the less rich and the least enterprising. They did not belong to the group of important entrepreneurs, the monopolists and war profiteers. The majority were drawn from the second rank of the Canadian capitalist bourgeoisie. Without any great influence, their limited financial resources and their rather mediocre personal abilities had not allowed them to rise to the first rank in the busi-

ness world. Besides, they had not benefitted from official protection, not being part of the privileged group . . .

One can imagine their sigh of relief when the conqueror proclaimed that commerce would be free. This word, "liberty", was capable of fascinating them . . .

A memoir by the New Subjects, drawn up on the first of May 1765, accuses the French government of having impeded the progress of the colony by refusing to adopt "*la tolérance* [*liberté*]." The petitioners envied the "neighbouring colonies" which had benefitted by a policy inspired by "a concern for the general welfare . . . "

The illusion continued. Having become members of a rich and mighty empire the Canadian businessmen who remained in the country believed that they would be in a position to make attractive profits. They imagined . . . that the new colonial administration, advised by themselves, would watch paternally to promote their interests. They refused to take account of the fact that the Conquest had placed them in a greater state of inferiority than they had suffered during the last years of the French regime. Many great disappointments awaited them. . . .

A series of misfortunes descended upon them. The bankruptcy of the French government partially ruined the Canadian businessmen. Bills of Exchange drawn upon the public treasury and paper money constituted nearly the whole of their liquid capital. They recovered only a small part of it. We do not know exactly how much they lost by this unhappy chance. No one denies that the losses they suffered aggravated their already precarious situation. Their correspondence with their European suppliers and their petitions to the British government revealed all their distress at the thought that they would not be repaid in full. . . .

Fate continued to work increasingly against the Canadian merchants. Many of them had placed large orders in France during the war. The merchandise had not been delivered. At the moment when normal commerce was re-established after the capitulation of Montreal, their stores were empty. They took desperate steps to obtain permission from the British authorities to receive the goods they had ordered before the end of hostilities in America. These purchases had tied up the little credit they possessed. Without goods they could not re-establish their businesses that had been arrested by the war. The situation was truly alarming . . . Their representations and supplications were without success. The British government refused to allow French vessels to transport these goods to Canada and claimed that it was impossible for English ships to deliver them.

This decision of the British authorities did not favour the Canadian merchants. However, it was certainly not contrary to the interests of the English businessmen established in the conquered colony. Their London suppliers also found it to their profit. As to the *Canadien* bourgeoisie . . . their protestations of absolute loyalty had not had the results they expected. . . .

As in the past, the merchants could not pay cash for the merchandise which they imported. Their European suppliers had to agree to generous advances. Moreover, it is difficult to conceive of a commerce of any importance operating without recourse to credit. The Conquest had closed to the Canadian merchants their old markets where they had received credit and the goods they required. It took them some time to realize what was happening to them, for they tried for a long time to re-establish their commercial relations with France . . .

The Canadian merchants saw their profits diminishing. Several became unable to meet their obligations . . . St. Georges Dupré saw everything darkly: "If God abandons me I will quickly put an end to a life of greatest misfortunes."

Was the colony in a depression? On the contrary. From 1765 to 1771 the commerce of Canada knew years of abundance . . .

The Canadian businessmen had shown themselves incapable of standing up to their English competitors. The Conquest had exposed them to a competition with unequal weapons. This is the fact that dominates the whole of the economic history of the French Canadians since the Conquest . . .

. . . The present-day historian of French Canada sees what the Canadian leaders at the end of the eighteenth century did not see. . . . He sees that the *Canadiens*, barred from *haut commerce*, were unable to acquire the habits of big business. Kept in a minority and in subordinate positions in the public administration, they were deprived of obtaining government positions and of developing political traditions. The Canadian nation, thirty years after the Conquest, no longer possessed the framework necessary for the normal development of an Atlantic community. This was one of the results of the Conquest: a sociological phenomenon in no way due to the malignant designs of men. This colonial populace had lost its nourishing metropolis prematurely. Reduced to its own resources, it was destined to an anaemic collective survival. It would no longer benefit from the enlightened and dynamic direction of an economically independent bourgeoisie, totally devoted to its interests as an ethnic group and capable of building for itself a political, economic, social and cultural order exclusively for its benefit. There remained to it only a few institutions of secondary importance . . .

The absence of that secular and bourgeois directing class, whose rôle has been so important for the development of the societies of the Atlantic world, remains the great fact of the history of French Canada since the Conquest. . . . It will require long and patient researches to reveal all the terrible consequences of the displacement of the Canadian bourgeoisie. . . .

Michel Brunet, *French Canada and the Early Decades of British Rule, 1760-1791*, (Ottawa, The Canadian Historical Association, 1963), pp. 3-8. Reprinted by permission of the Canadian Historical Association.

The Conquest

Hypothesis Applied

The Capitulation of Montreal (September 8, 1760), which as Professor A. L. Burt remarks, should be called the Capitulation of Canada, fulfilled the hopes of the most ambitious leaders of the New England colonies and of the British empire. After a ruthless struggle lasting more than seventy years, the Anglo-Americans had triumphed. France and the Canadians could not obstruct any further the expansion of British colonization in North America.

Both in London and in the American colonies, great rejoicing welcomed Amherst's victory. From that moment, the leading political figures, both in the colonies and at home, worked to convince their compatriots and the imperial government that it was vital to retain Canada. Certain British statesmen and business men would have preferred the acquisition of Guadeloupe. There were two opposing conceptions of the British empire: that of a narrow mercantilism, according to which colonies only existed for commerce, and that which envisaged the growth of new Englands abroad, firmly linked to their metropolis. Those who dreamed of an Anglo-Saxon North America defeated the mercantilists.

MILITARY OCCUPATION OR THE RETURN OF PEACE

Although the war had ended on the American continent, it still continued for some months both in Europe and in India. The conclusion of the Family Compact between the different branches of the Bourbons—French, Spanish and Neapolitan (1761)—encouraged some Canadians to think that Spanish help would reverse the situation. These hopes were quickly cut short. As early as the summer of 1762, although a few might still imagine that France would recover the St. Lawrence Valley, the majority seemed to have become accustomed to the idea that the British would remain, at least for several years. However, the Canadians of the first generation after the Conquest, while submitting to British rule, always held the dream that France had not said her last word in North America. When the hour of revenge came, their former mother country would be able to rely upon them. Meanwhile, they bore their lot with resignation.

The judicious conduct of the British authorities greatly helped to reconcile the Canadians to the new regime. Amherst, Murray, Gage, Burton and Haldimand were prudent administrators, careful to reassure a population which had expected the worst. Official French propaganda had repeatedly stated that defeat would mean terror. But the measures taken by the military commanders aided a rapid return to normal daily life. The militia captains continued to exercise their former functions, the tribunals established by the victors rendered justice according to the established laws of the colony, the clergy had freedom to attend to the spiritual needs of the faithful, trade regained its former vigour. The inhabitants of the colony had only one thought: to profit from the return of peace to repair the damages of war.

The long conflict had left behind it much destruction and a general apathy. The death of Bishop Pontbriand, four months before the Capitulation of Montreal, placed the clergy in a particularly delicate situation. Bigot's administration as Intendant had made the French regime very unpopular during its last years. The bankruptcy of Louis XV's government, which had only redeemed a portion of the paper money and bonds drawn on the public treasury, had increased the chaos and augmented the discontent of the population. The victors had before them an exhausted populace, ready to be governed. All circumstances and factors helped to render the establishment of British rule easy.

THE KING IS DEAD—LONG LIVE THE KING!

French Canadians showed in general no astonishment when they learned of the ratification of the Treaty of Paris. The clergy and the middle class hurried to acclaim the new king given them by the fortunes of war. At that period the prestige of monarchical institutions was of a kind that those living in the second half of the twentieth century find difficult to understand. For the Canadian leaders of the eighteenth century, the king was the source and symbol of all power. Society, they thought, could not exist without monarchy, which they believed sincerely to be the will of God. This idea formed part of the mental equipment of the principal societies of the North Atlantic world.

Under such circumstances, the support of monarchy formed a rallying point and a bond between the leaders of all western countries. The historian must take this factor into account when he observes the behaviour and reactions of the clergy and the leading spokesmen of the Canadians on the morrow of the Conquest.

The *élite* of Canadian society showed a spirit of open collaboration with the victors. Immediately after the surrender of Quebec and Montreal, several young girls married officers of the victorious army. A few people were shocked but they represented the opinion of a minority. Canon Briand, grand vicar of the district of Quebec, ordered prayers to be said for George III at mass, even though the peace negotiations had not been concluded. To those who expressed astonishment at his decision he replied that the British "are our masters; and we owe to them what we owed to the French when they ruled." The Treaty of Paris could only confirm the leaders of Canadian society in their desire to collaborate with the British authorities. In any case, as long as they continued to live in the colony, they had no opportunity to do otherwise.

EMIGRATION AND THE DECAPITATION OF SOCIETY

Canadians of the upper class, who refused to submit to the victors, emigrated. They foresaw that their personal future was compromised in a colony where the principal channels of social promotion would, in future, be occupied by the British. The former administrators did not have to rack their brains overlong to discover who would succeed them. The most powerful business men understood that their enterprises would not prosper within the British commercial system.

It is true that some of these emigrants were forced to return to France in order to account for their administration and their scandalous fortunes. Nevertheless, only a few of those who left Canada were functionaries and traders guilty of embezzlement. The majority was drawn from honourable families who did not wish to suffer the humiliation of foreign occupation and who wanted to keep all the advantages which the French empire provided: royal pensions, access to public office, business relations with the capitalists of the metropolis, official protection, contracts with the government and so on. It has been calculated that at least two thousand Canadians left their native land during the ten years which followed the surrender of Montreal.

Can one speak about the loss of social leadership? Some historians, building upon the fact that the emigration of the ruling class was not overwhelming, maintain that Canadian society retained its form. Have they asked themselves what became of the former leaders who remained in Canada? Their fall, which was inevitable in a vanquished colony where a new body of administrators and executives of British origin was being assembled, is the most striking social phenomenon of the first generation after the Conquest. Canadian society no longer offered its most ambitious and dynamic members either the opportunity or the means to win prestige in public life. During the French colonial era, no career was closed to the Canadians. The French empire counted upon their help to continue and prosper. The situation was completely different under British rule. The administration, the army, the navy and external trade were all preserves of the British. The Canadians could not meet the competition of newcomers who came as conquerors. It could not be otherwise.

The Canadians had to learn to limit their ambitions and their horizons, which shrank to fit their diminished chances of social success. Deprived of the indispensable backing of its mother country, left to its own resources, submitting to the rule of a foreign upper class, French Canada lived in a state of subordination.

HOPES AND DREAMS OF THE CANADIANS

For the majority of the population there was no question of emigration. Faithful to the monarchic ideal, they recognized George III without protest as their new sovereign. However, in giving their allegiance to the king of Great Britain, the Canadians had no intention of renouncing the right to define and protect their own interests. The clergy, conforming to the traditional teaching of the Church, were ready to have *Te Deum's* sung to celebrate the peace and to do homage to "the legitimate authority". At the same time, they counted on the latter for the nomination of a bishop and the freedom to exercise their ministry. The seigneurs and the Canadian officers, to whom the defeat meant loss of prestige in the eyes of the habitants and the militia, deluded themselves into thinking that the British government, following the example of Louis XV, would have recourse to them for the administration and defence of the colony.

The Canadian business men, delighted by the departure of Bigot, his associates and favourites, hoped to improve their lot quickly. Had they not been told that the colony, thanks to its entry into the British market and to the freedom of trade which the English practised, would experience soaring prosperity? They had, for a few short years, the *naïveté* to imagine that they would be the principal beneficiaries of this upsurge of economic activity. They were soon to realize that their British competitors were basically the only ones equipped to benefit from it. Also, the middle-class Canadian traders who remained in the colony, influenced by the British business men who were coming in, had convinced themselves they would supplant the seigneurs in the social hierarchy.

As to the lowest strata, that is to say the immense majority of the population, what did they think? First of all, there was a strong impression of having been betrayed by those in authority. The latter suddenly appeared as being unworthy of their honours, their privileges and their responsibilities. In all societies, the immediate consequence of an unsuccessful war is a loss of authority and prestige by the former governing class. This particular group, however, as well as having been defeated on the battlefield, had to suffer occupation by the victorious army and had to collaborate with it, and thus lost even the possibility of regaining popular support. But the Canadians had no other leaders to whom they could give their loyalty. Obedient to both their seigneurs and clergy, they echoed "Long live the king!" At the same time, they took refuge in a state of passive resistance. Both the British authorities and the Canadian leaders realized this when an attempt was made to raise a volunteer battalion to help suppress Pontiac's rising (1764). The militia, in spite of alluring promises, showed no haste to enroll. The people, although submitting themselves to George III, felt no obligation to serve the interests of their enemies and conquerors. Sooner or later, they thought, the "Londoners", the English, would be forced to quit the country.

THE FAILURE OF THE ROYAL PROCLAMATION

A royal proclamation of October 7, 1763, announced that Canada, along with other new British colonies, was to have an elected assembly and that its inhabitants could expect "the enjoyment of the benefits of the laws of . . . England". General James Murray, who had been military governor since October 1759, was appointed civil governor of the colony, now called the Province of Quebec. His instructions (December 7, 1763) provided for a council including, besides officials, eight of the "most considerable" residents of the colony appointed on his recommendation. Murray was instructed to honour the treaty guarantee of religious toleration, but not to allow any papal or "any other foreign ecclesiastical jurisdiction whatever". He was also to have vacant lands surveyed in townships and to publish regulations for granting land in English tenure, the grantees to pay quit-rents. Quebec, in fact, was to be remade into an English colony. This programme, intended to attract immigrants from the comparatively crowded English colonies to the south, simply did not face the fact that the Canadians formed more than ninety-nine per cent of the white population in the St. Lawrence valley.

Murray, sympathetic to the Canadians but obedient and unimaginative, attempted to obey his instructions impartially. The result was the total disorganization of justice. The Canadians were delivered into the hands of judges and officials who were ignorant or contemptuous of their language and traditions, and some of whom exploited them shamelessly. The governor tried to set limits to the havoc by recognizing the right of Canadians to jury service and by creating lower courts. In them the judges were to take notice of French laws and customs and Canadian lawyers (who, being Catholic, could not practise in the Court of King's Bench) were allowed to represent their clients. This concession to the "natives", however, was stated to be only temporary.

Those who could legitimately regard themselves as the leaders of the Canadian community discovered, not without astonishment, that they had no public rights in their own country. The Test Act barred them, as Catholics, from careers in the administration, whether as councillors or as mere justices of the peace. They were totally ignorant of the English law which now replaced their own. Surely, they thought, their willingness to collaborate and their protestations of loyalty to the Crown merited greater consideration than this?

Murray, realizing that the number of British colonists was too small, decided to postpone the election of an assembly. This brought him the enmity of the group one can call the English party. The British merchants and adventurers who had come to Canada immediately after the Conquest expected, for the most part, to become its ruling class. They had been patient during the military regime, but they regarded the establishment of civil government (which came into force on August 10, 1764), as the beginning of their triumph. They had expected to dominate the assembly which Murray now postponed and to control both the Canadians and the officials sent out from Great Britain. They expressed their dis-

appointment in a manifesto of the Grand Jury of Quebec (October 16, 1764) and in petitions sent direct to Westminster. Murray, in response, moved closer to the Canadian leaders and defended them before the imperial government. At the same time, he was plagued by the hostility of the military commanders, who were themselves also at odds with the spokesmen of the British mercantile community.

Some members of the British minority were well-disposed towards the Canadians, and formed a political group called the "French party". The most influential of these advocates of paternalism was Adam Mabane, a Scottish surgeon who in 1764 was appointed a judge and a member of the governor's council. With this support and with Murray's, the Canadians demanded from the imperial government the redress of their grievances.

The British ministers had begun to doubt the wisdom of their policy towards His Majesty's new subjects in the Province of Quebec. Since they had no intention of persecution, deportation or liquidation, they were forced, while guarding the fundamental interests of the British empire, to take into account the presence of the Canadians. They were willing, for example, to accept a bishop recognized by Rome and consecrated in France. Canon Briand, who had been one of the vicars-general chosen to govern the diocese after Bishop Pontbriand's death, was allowed after several months' waiting in London to seek consecration discreetly. In June 1766 he returned as the head of the Canadian clergy. In the same month Murray, who had been recalled, left Quebec.

Jean Hamelin, *Économie et Société en Nouvelle-France*, (Québec, Les Presses Universitaires Laval, 1960), pp. 127-137. (Translated C.N.) Reprinted by permission of the Author.

The Conquest

Hypothesis Denied

Much has been written about the French Canadian bourgeoisie before 1760. Its origins have been traced to the formation of the *Compagnie des Habitants* in 1645; the Conquest was responsible for its decadence. A part of this bourgeoisie then emigrated to France, and the remainder, cut off from its economic bases (the fisheries and trading posts) by the revision of the boundaries of New France, died of suffocation. Thus, the annihilation of the French Canadian bourgeoisie in 1760 became the great historical event which dominates and determines the economic development of French Canada until Confederation.

The thesis is seductive, but does it correspond to the exact reality? It is permissible to ask this question, for the hypothesis has been advanced without any exhaustive research to support it. Hence the dossier is not closed; it is open for discussion. . . .

The essential fact . . . that is evident from the correspondence of the *Intendants,* is the poverty of the group of mer-

chants and traders, and this throughout the French regime. . . .

There is nothing in our research that entitles us to speak of a French Canadian bourgeoisie before 1760, and even less of an upper bourgeoisie, in the strict meaning of the term. Without doubt the explanation of this economic and social weakness is complex. It would distort reality to want to reduce it to a few simple factors. . . . There are, it seems to us, some permanent causes that must be evaluated.

Primarily we find an absence of well-to-do immigrants. That, we believe, was one of the principal causes. While English immigrants pouring into New England included bourgeois and merchants who brought their commercial traditions and capital with them, the French immigrants, on the contrary, contained as a general rule, only a few well-to-do persons. . . . From the economic point of view, one must regret that the metropolis did not, after the Revocation of the Edict of Nantes, direct the exodus of Protestants towards her North American colony, where they could have turned to profit their experience in commerce, their knowledge of crafts, and could have made their capital productive.

Further, did not the very nature of commerce in the colony impede the formation of a bourgeoisie? Was not the emigration of a portion of the merchants in 1760, which is represented as a new phenomenon, merely the repetition of a recurrent phenomenon, or the manifestation of a continuing process which, by force of the exceptional circumstances, attained a greater magnitude in 1760? Metropolitan merchants came to enrich themselves and return, their fortunes made. . . . The evil existed from the beginning of the colony. . . .

These reflections on the Canadian merchants may be challenged. They must be checked and verified by a study of private archives and notarial records. But even now can we not presume that the emigration of a few merchants in 1760, and the ruin of those who remained in the colony—if ruin there was—is only one aspect of a more profound problem? In fact, let us suppose there was established in the colony an upper bourgeoisie, masters of commerce, owning lucrative industries: what would have happened? They would not have emigrated. Did the *habitant*, who had his land, emigrate? Most of those who did emigrate were agents or associates of metropolitan companies, foreign temporary merchants, administrators who traded, *Canadiens* whose activities were dependent on those of French merchants, and suppliers of the military. The absence of a vigorous French Canadian bourgeoisie in 1800 thus appears a result of the French Regime, not a consequence of the Conquest. For the drama of French colonization in Canada was its inability to form a French Canadian bourgeoisie based on the rational exploitation of the natural resources of the country. . . .

Serge Gagnon, "Pour une conscience historique de la Révolution Québecoise", (*Cité Libre*, vol. XVI, no. 83, 1966), pp. 15-16. (Translated C.N.) Reprinted by permission of the Author.

Fernand Ouellet versus

the *Nationalistes*

. . . By his numerous articles Fernand Ouellet has acquired the reputation of a specialist on the first century following the Conquest. Like Hamelin, his researches have been in social and economic history. A fact to note is that his interpretation of the English Regime is very similar to that of Creighton.

The evolution of French Canada after the Conquest seems, on the whole, like a prolongation of the French Regime. It is an error to believe that the change of allegiance deprived the colony of its upper bourgeoisie. Rather, the latter is "a projection of neo-nationalist historiography." Indeed, several factors negated the possibility of the formation of such an elite group in New France. The despotic monarchy, the control of the fur trade by administrators, and the absence of a capitalist mentality were the principal causes.

To Ouellet, not only did the Conquest have no direct bearing upon the economic weakness of French Canada, but it was even a blessing in that it opened the markets of the [British] Empire to the wheat production of the colony. Thus our food products finally found a market that France had been unable to furnish. As for the fur trade, the *Canadiens* continued to play a predominant rôle until the American Revolution, at which time, little by little, the Scots displaced the *Canadiens*. This reversal of the situation, however, was not attributable to the presence of new competitors. Rather, it was owing to the deficiencies of our commercial bourgeosie confronted by a growing capitalism. The *Canadiens* at that time hesitated to undertake large enterprises and to diversify their investments. Furthermore, their mania for ostentation, an atavism of the French Regime, kept them from re-investing their profits. This in part explains why, at the beginning of the XIXth century, we see a decline of the French Canadian commercial bourgeoisie to the benefit of the English-speaking commercial class.

Indeed, as the fur trade declined, commercial capitalism tended to become identified with this [English-speaking] group. Thus the export of lumber during the Napoleonic Wars became almost entirely an activity of English capital. Now, if we look for the basic reasons for this decline, we are led to the conclusion that they all point to a refusal to adjust to new economic structures. The prime cause for this refusal was the retention of a type of traditional education hermetically sealed to bourgeois values. The absence of dynamic businessmen, of specialized labour, of farmers cognisant of modern agricultural techniques, necessitated furthermore the implementation of an educational system which would accord with the economic necessities of the period. But in the first half of the XIXth century the primary school did not develop along these lines. As for higher education, none existed. There had been the university project of 1789, sustained by the English bourgeoisie, but the non-confessional and neutral character they desired for it led to its rejection by the Catholic episcopate....

. . . the establishment of [classical] colleges stimulated the proliferation of professional men. Forming too large a group for the needs of the milieu, this elite believed that its prestige and security were linked with the achievement of political power. Shaped by its rural antecedents and upbringing, it could not dream of making common cause with the English-speaking commercial bourgeoisie. That is why, as the Rebellion [of 1837] drew nearer, it attempted to extend its power to the Legislative Assembly where, under the banner of liberal ideas, it defended its group interests by becoming the spokesmen for the discontented peasant class. . . .

Suggestions for Further Readings

Canadian historical literature, though respectable in volume, is less notable for its seminal content. There is no period, no subject, no individual studied to date that cannot be again researched, and with much profit. All too often one book, and but one, exists on a topic. Or, what is perhaps worse, the interpretations of a subject vary little from historical generation to historical generation. What follows is a listing and comment on some sources suggested for further consideration of the topics covered in this booklet.

Many references are made to the nature of Canadian society during the French regime. Apart from those used in this booklet, valuable information may be found in Guy Fregault's *Canadian Society During the French Regime*, (Ottawa, Canadian Historical Association, 1956, 16 pp.); Cameron Nish, *The French Regime*, (Toronto, Prentice-Hall of Canada, 1965, 176 pp.); and the same author's "Une bourgeoisie coloniale en Nouvelle-France: Une hypothèse de travail," (*L'Actualité Economique*, juillet-septembre, 1963, pp. 240-265). S. D. Clark's *The Social Development of Canada*, (Toronto, University of Toronto Press, 1942, 484 pp.) is also a valuable work, and includes documents.

Manuscript sources on the period 1759 to 1766 abound. The more important collections in the Public Archives of Canada are listed in the *Preliminary Inventory, Manuscript Group 23, Late Eighteenth Century Papers*, (Ottawa, Queen's Printer, 1957, 52 pp.). A listing of the calendars of the P.A.C. collections has been offprinted as *A Guide to the Calendars, Registers and Descriptive Lists of Series and Collections in the Public Archives*, (Ottawa, King's Printer, 1950, pp. 451-462). The most important printed sources, apart from the Shortt and Doughty selection of *Constitutional Documents* used in this work, will be found in the publications of the Report of the Public Archives of Canada. The *Archives du Québec* have recently published a cumulative table of contents listing their publications since 1920: *Table des Matières des Rapports des Archives du Québec, Tomes I à 42, (1920-1964)*, (Québec, Roch Lefebvre, 1965, 104 pp.). This is a very valuable guide to original documents printed in the R.A.Q.

Any number of standard works may be consulted with profit, apart from those cited above. Bruchesi's *A History of Canada*, published originally in French as *Histoire du Canada, nouvelle édition*, (Montréal, Beauchemin, 1951, 682 pp.), is the approach of a moderate *nationaliste*. A not so moderate, yet not separatist, approach is evident in Canon Lionel Groulx's: *Histoire du Canada Français depuis la Découverte, 4e. édition*, (Montréal, Fides, 1960, Volume 1). There is, as yet, no overtly separatist History of Canada, or of Quebec. There does now exist, however, a *vue d'ensemble*, a plan of the courses of Maurice Séguin of the *Université de Montréal*. It will be found on pp. 224-234 of Denis Vaugeois' *L'Union des Deux Canada: Nouvelle Conquête, 1791-1840*, (Trois-Rivières, Editions du Bien Public, 1962, 241 pp.). Among historians writing in English, Mason Wade's *The French Canadians, 1860-1945*, (Toronto, Macmillan Company, 1956, 1136 pp.) should be consulted. A classic 'Whig' interpretation of Canadian history will be found in William Kingsford's *The History of Canada*, Volumes IV and V, (Toronto, Rowsell & Hutchison, 1890-1892). Of a later date, but in much the same vein, is H. E. Egerton's *A Historical Geography of the British Colonies, Volume V: Canada, Part II: Historical*, (Oxford, Clarendon Press, 1908, 365 pp.). Other standard texts are those of W. L. Morton, Edgar McInnis, J. M. S. Careless, D. G. Creighton, and the recently

published work of R. Cook, J. Saywell and J. C. Ricker.

Economic history, still a much avoided subject in Canadian historical literature, may be garnered from a few works. Easterbrook and Aitken's *Canadian Economic History*, (Toronto, MacMillan Company, 1956, 606 pp.) is one of the few general works on the subject. H. A. Innis' books and articles are still the prime source, in particular his *The Fur Trade in Canada*, rev. ed., (Toronto, University of Toronto Press, 1956, 463 pp.).

Imperial-colonial relations are well covered by several works. G. L. Beer's *British Colonial Policy, 1754-1765*, (Gloucester, Mass., Peter Smith, 1958, 327 pp.), originally published in 1907, is a must. L. H. Gipson's *The Coming of the Revolution, 1763-1775*, (New York, Harper & Row, 1962, 287 pp.), and K. E. Knorr's *British Colonial Theories, 1570-1850*, (Toronto, University of Toronto Press, 1944, 429 pp.) may both be read with profit.

One of the better works in a field as yet unexplored is l'Abbé A. Gosselin's *L'Eglise du Canada Après la Conquête, Première Partie, 1760-1775*, (Québec, Imprimerie Laflamme, 1916, 432 pp.). Less satisfying is Lionel Groulx's book on the same subject.

Periodical articles are among the best sources of further readings on the topic of the Conquest and the early years of British rule. H. R. Balls, "Quebec, 1763-1774: The Financial Administration," (*Canadian Historical Review*, vol. XLI, 1960, pp. 203-214); Duncan McArthur, "The British Board of Trade and Canada, 1760-1774, 1: The Proclamation of October, 1763," (*Canadian Historical Association Report*, 1922, pp. 97-113); S. Morley Scott, "Civil and Military Authority in Canada, 1764-1766," (*Canadian Historical Review*, vol. LX, 1928, pp. 117-136); A. L. Burt, "The Mystery of

Walker's Ear," (*Canadian Historical Review*, vol. III, 1922, pp. 233-255); and M. G. Reid's "The Quebec Fur-Traders and Western Policy, 1763-1774," (*Canadian Historical Review*, vol. VI, 1926, pp. 15-32), are excellent essays.

Further development of the Brunet-Ouellet controversy may be garnered from Fernard Ouellet's "M. Brunet et le problème de la Conquête," (*Bulletin des Recherches Historiques*, vol. 62, 1956, pp. 92-101), and his "Les Fondements historiques de l'option séparatiste dans le Québec," (*Canadian Historical Review*, vol. XLIII, 1962, pp. 185-203). A very thorough examination of Ouellet's position is contained in his doctoral thesis presented at *l'Université Laval* in 1965. It is to be published by Fides, of Montreal, in the Fall of 1966. Brunet's views, apart from those presented in this booklet, are evident in his "Les Canadiens après la Conquête: Les débuts

de la résistance passive," (*Revue de l'Histoire de l'Amérique Française*, vol. XII, 1958, pp. 170-207) and "The British Conquest: Canadian Social Scientists and the Fate of the *Canadiens*," (*Canadian Historical Review*, vol. XL, 1958, pp. 93-107).

Two historiographical essays on the problem of the Conquest and its historians are worthy of consideration: Ramsay Cook's "L'Historien et le Nationalisme: Le Cas Michel Brunet," (*Cité Libre*, vol. 15, 1965, pp. 5-14), is one. The extract from Serge Gagnon cited in this booklet is drawn from a general survey of the schools of interpretation of Laval and Montreal. In it he presents the positions of the major and minor figures in the controversy. His "Pour une conscience historique de la Révolution Québecoise," (*Cité Libre*, vol. 16, 1966, pp. 4-16), while lacking in subtlety, is, at the moment, the best general survey of the problem.

5 6 7 8 9 — 76 75 74 73 72